In Richard's World

SOUTHERN CLASSICS SERIES

Mark M. Smith, Series Editor

In Richard's World

The Battle of Charleston
1966

With a New Introduction by the Author

William H. Barnwell

The University of South Carolina Press

*Published in Cooperation with the Institute for
Southern Studies of the University of South Carolina*

Cloth edition published by Hougton Mifflin, 1968
Paperback edition published by the University of South Carolina Press,
Columbia, South Carolina 29208
www.sc.edu/uscpress

Manufactured in the United States of America

22 21 20 19 18 17 16 15 14 13
10 9 8 7 6 5 4 3 2 1

Library of Congress Cataloging-in-Publication Data
Barnwell, William Hazzard, 1938–
In Richard's world : the battle of Charleston, 1966 : with a
new introduction by the author / William H. Barnwell.
pages cm. — (Southern classics series)
Originally published: Boston : Houghton Mifflin, 1968.
ISBN 978-1-61117-248-5 (pbk. : alk. paper) 1. African Americans—South
Carolina—Charleston—Social conditions—20th century. 2. African Americans—
Civil rights—South Carolina—Charleston—History—20th century. 3. Civil rights
movements—South Carolina—Charleston—History—20th century. 4. Charleston
(S.C.)—Social conditions—20th century. 5. Charleston (S.C.)—Race relations—
History–20th century. 6. Barnwell, William Hazzard, 1938– I. University of South
Carolina. Institute for Southern Studies, issuing body. II. Title.
F279.C49N413 2013
305.896'0730757915—dc23
2012046818

The afterword is from *Lead Me On, Let Me Stand,*
by William Barnwell, copyright 2012 by Andover Press
(andoverbooks.com). Reprinted with permission.

Publication of the Southern Classics series is made possible in part
by the generous support of the Watson-Brown Foundation.

Contents

Series Editor's Preface

SOUTHERN CLASSICS returns to general circulation books of importance dealing with the history and culture of the American South. Sponsored by the Institute for Southern Studies, the series is advised by a board of distinguished scholars who suggest titles and editors of individual volumes to the series editors and help establish priorities in publication.

Chronological age alone does not determine a title's designation as a Southern Classic. The criteria also include significance in contributing to a broad understanding of the region, timeliness in relation to events and moments of peculiar interest to the American South, usefulness in the classroom25, and suitability for inclusion in personal and institutional collections on the region.

William H. Barnwell's new introduction to his memoir, *In Richard's World: The Battle of Charleston, 1966*, reminds us, powerfully, of the "stomach-clutching question" facing so many white southerners during the civil rights movement. In this candid, touching, and at times highly poignant treatment, Barnwell explores how many people in Charleston in the 1960s answered that pressing, emotional, and fraught question. *In Richard's World* charts the struggles and ordeals of African Americans, details the challenges facing white liberals living in the South, and wrestles with an issue fundamental to the process of desegregation: "How can you love your own people and yet fight them at the same time on the great question of race?" Barnwell's compelling exploration of this question makes this a very welcome addition to the Southern Classics series.

MARK M. SMITH
Series Editor

Preface

WHEN I RETURNED to Virginia Theological Seminary in September of 1966 to complete my last year of study for the Episcopal ministry, I read the following words in our school catalog:

> There is no way of predicting just where in the course of study a man will "come alive" and say in effect, "So that's what it's all about! This is for me." The shape of the curriculum and the forms of common life at Virginia express the intention that somewhere along the line a man will say just that.

It occurred to me that for the first time I was ready to say, "Christianity and perhaps even the ministry are for me." I had just completed a summer of work in a Negro mission center in Charleston, South Carolina, my home town.

Working by day in the world of a Negro ghetto and living at night in the world of what's left of our old Southern society, I realized that I would have to express my thoughts — on paper — in order to retain any objectivity at all. I thus began keeping a diary in a frantic effort to make sense out of my two conflicting worlds. My first rule was honesty. I had to be honest with myself if I was to be able to look on *myself* with any degree of objectivity. So, if I felt like cursing, I cursed. If I felt like being ruthless, I was — at least on paper. If I felt joy, I tried to convey that.

Why publish this diary? What value will my personal experience be to the general reader? My story is about a few insignificant people who live in a town you don't hear much about any more. And besides that, I'm not particularly experienced in race relations, social science, or even Christianity.

I wanted to publish this diary because my summer did make me "come alive." And I simply want to tell people about it, about how the Bible suddenly spoke to me, how my seminary training grabbed hold of me, how, for a short while, the rhythm of my life became the rhythm of the Bible. I was at last at home as a Christian. Day by day during the hot summer of 1966, I came to realize that life was meant to be a series of deaths and rebirths, of leaving one homeland and entering another.

The strength of the Bible is that it teaches and proclaims through narrative. It says in effect, "If you want to know about God and the nature of things, let me tell you this story." I've tried to tell *my* story in this book with a minimum of "theologizing." In the book, I describe water games on a certain picnic rather than speak of "baptism by the Holy Ghost." I write about a big dance instead of writing about "resurrection experiences." I shout "Goddam" instead of speaking of "ultimate anxiety" and "despair."

The summer of 1966 forced me to confront myself. The particular issue was the racial struggle. In it, I came alive. But that was in the summer of 1966. At the present time, I find myself in a new set of circumstances, with new threats, new hopes, new possibilities of death and rebirth. But that's another story. I often wonder how much I have changed on account of that summer experience. I suspect very little. I'm like the retarded boy, Richard, for whom this book is named. I do better for a while, come alive for a short while, then go back to my old ways. But it's those short periods that make the whole thing worthwhile.

Let me thank some of my teachers — Mr. A. Mays from high school days, Dr. Clifford Stanley and Dr. A. T. Mollegen from seminary days, and finally the many Negroes whom I came to know during the days of the summer of 1966. I hope this book is worthy of all of you. Let me also thank my two editors — Miss Shannon Ravenel of Houghton Mifflin who has given me the direction and encouragement I needed to complete this project and Dr. Richard Reid of Virginia Theological Seminary who painstakingly has gone over the manuscript with me, word by word.

In order to protect the privacy of certain individuals whom I've described, I have disguised them beyond recognition.

W. H. B.

Introduction

IN RECENT YEARS I have learned to be kind to the young man who wrote *In Richard's World: The Battle of Charleston, 1966*. For a long time, I blamed myself for trying to work out my problems relating to race among a group of people who never asked me to come work at their Episcopal community center in the first place. At my request, the bishop had assigned me, a seminarian, to work at St. John's (St. Paul's in the book) in the most dilapidated part of Charleston for that summer of 1966. If I was going into the Episcopal ministry, I had to figure out where I stood on race.

And then I was embarrassed that in the book I made such generalizations as "the Negro"—who *the* Negro was and what *he* wanted, needed. I was also embarrassed that I had admitted to personal prejudice at various times in the book, and at times may have made fun of the local black dialect, rich though it was. And, finally, I was embarrassed because I wrote *In Richard's World* not knowing very much about what was going on in the civil rights movement throughout the South. What, for example, did I know about the heroism of Freedom Riders in 1961 and the volunteers who came to Mississippi during Freedom Summer in 1964, or even the martyrdom of Jonathan Daniels, a fellow Episcopal seminarian (at another institution), killed in 1965 in Hayneville, Alabama?

One thing I'm sure of—I could never have written *In Richard's World* if I had waited a couple of years. By then, I was working on the edge of the civil rights movement as I also tried in 1967–68 to serve my first church, St. Paul's, in Conway, South Carolina, and then in 1969–70 my next church, St. Martin's-in-the-Fields in Columbia. I knew too much about what was going on in what then was called the moveMENT, with the accent on the last syllable, and my writing would have been inhibited.

In 1966 my writing was not inhibited, and that may be the lasting value of *In Richard's World.* I told it all: my pain at seeing such poverty; my amazement that even in a beaten-down slum—I was probably right to call it "a ghetto"—the people there could rise from their distress and, as one disc jockey said at a neighborhood dance, "live . . . live, man, live." I called that "resurrection in the midst of death." I told of the outright racism that I encountered when I sought help for those in great distress, physically and emotionally. I told of the blind and overwhelming (but not necessarily mean-spirited) prejudice of my closest family members and most of my friends.

As that long ago summer wore on, I realized that my main problem was not my racism, though I probably had plenty of that. My main problem was that "my" people, whom I dearly loved, who gave me everything in my growing-up years, were now becoming "the enemy." How can you love your own people and yet fight them at the same time on the great question of race?

That was the stomach-clutching question that so many of us white folk from the Deep South were asking in those turbulent years of the late fifties and sixties and into the seventies. Sure, we had to deal with our racism, whether hidden or overt, but the hardest questions related to our loyalties. Many so-called reconstructed Southerners, such as Willie Morris in his compelling book *North Toward Home,* had already arrived on the other side of what seemed like the River Jordan. And they wrote books, looking back on the difficult journey that carried them there.

In 1966, like so many of my white contemporaries in the Deep South, I had not arrived anywhere. I was dogpaddling *in* the River Jordan, my head slightly above the water, just trying to figure things out: by day, loving the children and adults I was getting to know at the community center; by night, hanging out with very close family and friends. Black by day, white by night. At the mission center, I worked endlessly to start new programs for young people of all ages. I took carloads of children and teens to swim at segregated beaches, and I also helped integrate Camp St. Christopher on Seabrook Island with five boys from the poorest homes in South Carolina.

At the end of each day, I sat in front of my father's World War II–era typewriter and wrote down just what happened, banging out my frustrations and anger—and love. That was my journal that eventually became *In Richard's World*. Richard was a "retarded" boy who hung out at the center, whom everyone loved but who could not seem to grow. (In those days, the word *retarded* was more descriptive than intentionally negative.) After that summer, I was becoming convinced that the world was like Richard.

Many things still stand out for me: how during our first softball game, a teenager, the first boy to get a hit—and it was a good one—ran to third base instead of first. How telling that was! I still think of how another boy, who had lived in Charleston all of his life, didn't understand about tides and thought an oyster bank "rose up" out of the water, and how Mrs. Martin, who fed all the children in Head Start, used her own meager income to feed anybody who was hungry. And I will always remember Mr. Freddie with his "bad heart" and no education. He just showed up one day to recruit for the Boy Scout Troop I was starting, and he told story after story to the delighted boys.

Mr. Freddie did most of his recruiting for me and for others and also his never-ending "ministerin'" on the street corners, where idle boys hung out, thinking up mischief (or worse) to get into. Once he told me, "The trouble with this city is that they's just too many street corners." He died before the summer was over. At his funeral— "home-going"—I compared Mr. Freddie to the widow who gave her pennies to the temple. Jesus said of her that she had given more than anyone else, for she gave everything she had—in one translation, "her whole living." Mr. Freddie was like that.

Shortly after the book was published, Mother called and said with a trembling voice, "Your father and I have read every word." A long pause. "William, how could you!" And then for the first time and the last time in my life, she hung up on me. I pictured my parents, elderly by then, propped up in the Old Charleston four-poster handed down through six or more generations—my mother reading aloud, my father because of a stroke not being able to read but taking in every word. His eyes are red from tears, his voice all choked up. How could his son, his boy, have done this to them, when they had given me everything?

I may have been too careful to give made-up names to the different places where the stories took place and different names to some of the characters. The name of the Episcopal Center was not St. Paul's but, as I've mentioned, St. John's. It has been converted into a lovely Episcopal Chapel and was dedicated, coincidently, on my birthday, October 12, 2009; they invited me to speak. The neighborhood is still poor but not so terribly poor as it was in 1966. Fr. Andrews in the book, my African American supervisor, was Father Henry Grant, who served the diocese for many years after I knew him, finally dying in 1985. St. Thomas Church was St. Philip's, my ancient growing-up church, and our rival church was St. Michael's. Richard was Richard, and Mr. Freddie was Mr. Freddie. I made no attempt to disguise myself—a collateral descendent of Robert Barnwell Rhett of the *Charleston Mercury*; he was a noisy and very influential advocate for the South Carolina Secession, which occurred December 20, 1860.

In my semiretired years, I find myself once again working, though part-time, in another largely African American community center and church, in the still-devastated Lower Ninth Ward of New Orleans, where Hurricane Katrina in 2005 caused the worst damage. Once again I report to an African American priest, Father Lonell Wright. After Katrina, Walgreen's gave its badly flooded drugstore in the Lower Ninth Ward to the Episcopal Diocese. Volunteers have made it over into a fine church and community center—All Souls, or, as some call it, St. Walgreen's. Once again I am experiencing resurrection—life—in the midst of death. And I am still writing. My latest book, *Lead Me On, Let Me Stand: A Clergyman's Story in White and Black*, was published in August 2012.

WILLIAM BARNWELL
October 12, 2012

I

The First Day

And at last, there we were on Broad Street, the
boundary between the buffer zone and the
pretty and historical part. The people who
live South of Broad are known as the "S.O.B.'s"
— because of their geographical location, of
course — by the rest of town. These are the
people who are sent away to prep school, then
to college, who then return to old Charleston
and never leave. They are my people.

DRIVING FROM NORTH TO SOUTH, from Arlington, Virginia, to Charleston, South Carolina, you have to pass through a lot of lonely, unpopulated swamp country as you come down through the Carolina lowcountry. By the time we reach this part of the trip, it is late afternoon; and since my wife is sleeping and my radio doesn't work, I drive and think about the past, drive and dream of the future. Occasionally, another car or a farmer in a truck will pass us going the other way, but mostly it's just us, us and those ancient cypress trees standing out there in that dark and stagnant water. It was here that Francis Marion, the Revolutionary War hero, led his men to hide after they had made raids on the British army; here he received the name Swamp Fox.

The day was June 10, 1966. On this particular trip I had more to meditate upon than usual. My wife and I were driving down from Virginia, where I am attending an Episcopal seminary, where she is teaching the first grade, to spend the summer in the place where I was raised. We were planning to live with my parents, and to run around with our old friends at night. During the day, I would be working at a church mission center in one of the worst slum areas in town — under a Negro priest. White Charleston by night, black Charleston by day; segregation at home, integration at work. Life among the Southern-gentleman cocktail set; life among those at the bottom of society. This was the specific work I had requested.

How in the world did I get myself into this kind of a situation? That was the question I kept asking myself as we drove along. I suppose my larger question was: Why, in the first place, did I leave my home in Charleston, where I had a good job in a bank, and go to seminary? I say that's the larger question because it was going to seminary that now had me involved in this present spot. Why does anyone go into the ministry? It's a rough question, one which we seminarians are constantly beset with, but a good question and one I answer differently each time.

Few if any of us ministerial students are fortunate enough to have a vision on the Road to Damascus, like St. Paul. Most are like me and go into the ministry for some selfish reason. Actually, this is my second attempt at seminary. I started out at this same school in 1961 but stayed only for one semester. Before entering that time, we had to write an essay telling why we wanted to study for the ministry. I remember that I told about an event from my recent past which had twisted and torn my insides, separating intellect from will, leaving me in the despair of the pit, in the confusion of battle, an event in which love and hate became confused. I told how this agony had almost caused me to drop out of Coast Guard Officer Candidate School the year before. And then I told how something I hadn't counted on saved me. "Time," I said, "is what did it," just the passage of time. Pascal wrote: "Time heals griefs and quarrels, for we change and are no longer the same persons. Neither the offender nor the offended are any more themselves."

Since *God* gave us time, I was able to thank him for my climbing out of the pit into the world of order. I had come a long way — I thought if I went into the ministry of the church and continued to sing God's praises I would be assured of overcoming my inner sicknesses permanently — but I had a long way to go. It had been a great mistake to confuse the organized church with God. Seminary did not turn out to be the healer that time had been. In fact, new events tore at me, new quarrels split me. I didn't tell anyone that I was leaving. One day, I just left. I didn't know why, not really.

I do know that the particular thing that caused me to leave was the struggle over race. I was reared a segregationist and never questioned my attitude until I came under the influence of an English teacher in a North Carolina prep school. At college, I would still take the segregationist point of view when I argued with "liberals"; but when I'd come home on vacation, I'd use the arguments of those liberal fellows to argue with my parents. And I got screaming mad no matter which way I was arguing.

The seminary was solidly committed to integration. In fact, the subject no longer seemed to be an issue. I agreed with the opinion of the place verbally but found myself rejecting it secretly. Each morning when I opened the door to my room, I opened it to face, right there in front of me in the hall of the dormitory, a huge poster of Jesus hanging on the cross, a barbed wire fence running through the middle of him. On one side of the fence he was black, and on the other he was white. So every morning before brushing my teeth I was reminded that I was not only crucifying Christ with my dark thoughts, but that I was also running him through with those grotesque wire prongs. And then there was a senior in the dorm who called me "Ree," for "reactionary conservative," because I once argued with him, the bastard, when he was damning the South, my homeland, in the most vicious way. Soon I began feeling those prongs in me, and I'm not Jesus, so I couldn't take it. Maybe I could have learned to become fully committed to the integrationist point of view — I was becoming quite friendly with a Negro student — but I could not imagine how I could ever become a brother of that senior, how I could go back home and preach race to the people I love, to the people who say they'll fight racial integration "until their dying day."

So one day, realizing that I was sliding back into my pit, I packed up my stuff and drove home. I had a lot of thinking to do that day as I crossed the South Carolina swamps, and I had no wife I could rouse from sleep if the thinking became too painful. Once back in Charleston, however, the conflict seemed to disappear, both the outward manifestation of it, my confused thoughts about the race question and the inner cause of it, whatever that was. I got a good job in a local bank, moved into a bachelors' apartment with some good-humored friends who hung posters of nude girls in the hall that made me tingle rather than hurt inside. Instead of talking race and salvation, we'd talk fishing and hunting. It was in this happy period of my life that I met my wife. We lost no time in getting married.

So there I was, good job, good friends, good wife. Why did I leave Charleston again? The question is more complex when you consider the hold that particular city has upon its native children, that city which may be described as a modern Greek city-state on which men ultimately rely, that city, self-sufficient Charleston, which not only influences our thinking but becomes a real part of our being. Why did I pull out? It was not to give myself to God that I left. It was not because I was any better than my bachelor friends that I left. I know that much.

Let me try to explain. The first time at seminary, though I mostly hated it from the time I opened the door of my room in the morning until I closed it at night, I did live for a short while completely within an atmosphere that was entirely different from old Charleston. As different as day is from night. While I re-adapted to Charleston life, I was at first able to put seminary out of my mind, but gradually a change came over me. Time was working its subtle ways on me once again. I came to find that I was more interested in teaching Sunday School than I was in working at the bank. Soon I was remembering only the good things about seminary. Sitting there in the bank, making automobile loans, laughing with customers who told me unfunny stories about niggers, nodding my head as though in agreement when they told me that the civil rights legislation was the result of communist infiltration, I would — sitting there at the desk — long for those days at seminary when I had a Negro friend, those days when the conversation, no matter how unpleasant, was important to me. Also, I began talking a lot about going back to seminary in the distant future. One day my wife said to me, "Now listen, either let's go back to seminary next year, or *shut up* about it."

We were back the next fall. That was in 1964. There were still a couple of those gruesome posters around; but we didn't have to live on campus, and besides I was more ready to listen to the seminary now. This time I found myself identifying more with that world than with the Charleston one, becoming in the process more and more committed to integration, at least intellectually. But just as a Jew never forgets he's a Jew, a Charlestonian never forgets where he's from. He must always have a relationship to *the* city — either a positive one, loving it, or a negative one, hating it, or both. I, being the kind of guy who always tries to do both — I love it and I hate it. So here I am — caught in a black-white, seminary-Charleston, love-hate conflict again, hung on that barbed wire fence, not yet cast into the pit but hurting inside.

One of the things they teach us at seminary nowadays is that Christ let himself be crucified, not so that we can climb down from the barbed wire fence, but so that we can have "the courage to be" in a hostile and threatening world.

I'm not entirely sure what that means, but it seems to mean at least this much — we must and we can face things as they are, even the most painful things that we don't understand and don't know how to handle. I really wasn't facing the race question either at the bank or at seminary; for in both situations, I was only talking about it, finding it too easy to switch point of view. Thus, when I heard about the job at the Negro mission center at home, I applied at once. By working in black Charleston and living in white Charleston, I would have to face the conflict concretely — I would have to deal with people, not merely ideas. I knew deep down that the conflict was probably insoluble, both the external racial conflict and the conflict within me. How can you live in two opposing worlds without choosing one and excluding the other? Are not both worlds apt to reject me? The white world seeing me as an enemy, the black world seeing me as a phony liberal, a person trying to work some personal thing out at their expense. Can you live in such a tension without dividing your personality, your personhood? Can you live *without* such a tension? Time, the one thing I hadn't counted on, saved me before. What I wondered, if anything, would pull me through this summer?

"Where are we?" my wife asked, sitting up in the car.

"We are leaving the land of the exile, and re-entering the land of milk and honey. The River Jordan is only a few miles away."

"What!"

"We are climbing back up on the barbed wire fence since there's nowhere else to go."

"Oh no, not *that* again," she said, turning over, closing her eyes, probably smiling to herself.

We were coming out of the swamp now, into some farm land. Along the side of the road, Negroes weave baskets with needles that are said to have been brought over from Africa by their ancestors and handed down through the generations. They tell me that racial relations in the country and in the small towns of lower South Carolina present a set of problems different from the ones that I would be dealing with. In Charleston, there is in the offing a battle between ghetto Negroes and the dwindling remains of the Southern aristocracy, both of whom are crowded together on one narrow peninsula. Out in the country and in the small towns, the white people resist change primarily because they are a conservative rural people. The Negroes, they tell me, show little interest in change for the same reason.

About the time you reach Mount Pleasant, the eastern suburb of the city, elevation fifteen feet, you begin to feel the ocean breeze and smell the pluff mud, which smells like dead fish to the outsider, but to us Charlestonians it's the perfume of heaven. Once an old maid great-aunt of mine who lived in Tennessee and had not returned to Charleston for some twenty years persuaded a cousin of ours to bring her a jar of pluff mud for her eightieth birthday. Several years later, a few weeks before she died, I saw that the jar was still there on the hall table, the smell gone, the mud hardened into rock.

Besides that Charleston smell, Mount Pleasant itself brings back some of my best boyhood memories. For the first twelve or thirteen years of my life, we left the city in the summertime and stayed with my grandparents on the Mount Pleasant waterfront. Every morning at four o'clock, my grandfather, who was retired, would take me fishing and shrimping with him in a homemade rowboat that had two bows. He'd wake me up with coffee made by what he called "the Bessemer Process," the kind you have to strain through your teeth to avoid swallowing the grounds, the kind you pour down the sink when your grandfather isn't looking. And so that I wouldn't go out on an empty stomach, he'd make me eat a bowl of hominy, not grits, but hominy! Then we'd get out there on the water and bring in the fish. One time, the story goes, we caught so many fish that we had to get out and push the boat. He nicknamed me Shipshape because I made such an unshapely mess of the fishing lines and the fish guts. Once I caught a catfish, which I carelessly flung into the boat and which, with its poisonous dorsal fin set, stuck upright in my bare foot. Grandfather knew the way to get the poison out. He spat tobacco juice on the place where the fin went in, then he made me take a shoe and beat out whatever poison wasn't absorbed by the tobacco. If you don't believe me, I'll show you the knot on my foot today to prove it. As we drove through Mount Pleasant toward the Cooper River, I wondered what my grand-father would think, if he were alive, about my working in a Negro mission center.

"Look," my wife said — waking up this time for good — when the twin three-mile Cooper River bridges came into sight, "they've completed the second bridge. Charleston sure is growing." From the top of the bridge, we could see the river on the other side of town, the Ashley River, which together with the Cooper River separates the peninsula from the main-land. Below us was the harbor. A Japanese ship was tied up to one dock, a Greek ship was approaching another while several tugs moved around it like sharks. A Negro was fishing in a small boat near the shoreline. Sailboats further out, reflecting the setting sun, seemed to be playing games, butterfly games, with each other. Way out in the harbor toward the jetties was Fort Sumter, the place where the war started, and the place where my teen-age crowd used to go on boat rides and picnics; that was, before the Yankees made it into a national monu-ment, renovating it, opening it to the public, ruining all the fun.

To the south of us was the city. The two steeples of St. Thomas' and St. Matthew's Episcopal churches at the far end of the peninsula always catch my eye. St. Matt's is painted white and was built first, but St. Tom's has that natural look to it and its congregation is much, much older. In fact, we argue that it founded St. Matt's as a mission long ago.

It is this southernmost tip of the peninsula that gives Charleston its luster; the rest of the city is drab. Between the Cooper River bridges and the Ashley River Bridge on the other side, there is a wide belt of slums. A buffer zone of middle class housing, of small stores of all sorts that are gradually going out of business in this shopping-center age, and of more slums, not quite so bad as the others, stretches between the bad slums and the pretty part of town. At the foot of the bridge, I thought about showing my wife the mission center, not far away.

I worked at that same center for a couple of months on Sunday afternoons the year before I returned to seminary. I was trying to get a Boy Scout troop started. I failed; and I hadn't driven by the center since that time. It is a place you don't just drive by, take a quick look at, and leave. It's on a street of decaying two- and three-story houses, a street with rubbish everywhere. Driving by, you find yourself setting your eyes on the few brightly painted houses and blinking them at the rest of the houses. That's easy to do. It is quite difficult, however, to blink your eyes at the swarms of half-dressed, dirty children who play in the street, the tired old men who sit in doorways — doing nothing, thinking nothing — the obese Negro women who talk and laugh loudly on the way home from work. I didn't go back for a quick look anytime after I quite working there; nor did I go back for a quick look my first day in Charleston.

Instead, we drove the two miles along the waterfront down the street that takes you to the lower tip of the city where my parents live. About halfway down that street there is an island of beauty amidst the ugliness of the slums. Some historic society backed certain people who wanted to renovate this small section of town that contains "many fine old houses" so that the slum dwellers wouldn't completely destroy them with their many children and their dirty and careless ways. In the language of the local newspaper, they converted this small section from an "eyesore" to a "beauty spot." Don't ask me what became of those people who irritated our sensitive eyes.

And at last, there we were on Broad Street, the boundary between the buffer zone and the pretty and historical part. The people who live South of Broad are known as the "S.O.B.'s" — because of their geographical location, of course — by the rest of town. These are the people who are sent away to prep school, then to college, who then return to old Charleston, and never leave. They are my people. I once heard this S.O.B. area described as a "small town within a large city."

Broad Street is also the main business street for the area, and it is here that I worked in the bank. It is also here that the Negroes, mostly high school youngsters, demonstrated by marching with signs several summers ago. The white people took the advice of the newspaper and pretended to ignore them, waiting for them to get tired of walking — which they did — then the whites went on about their business as usual. Those Negroes were not ignored, however, as much as they were led to believe. They were the topic of many conversations in Charleston board rooms and across dinner tables. The business world was worried that they might frighten away national industry, feeble as their one protest demonstration was. The social world laughed at them. Jokes such as one called "The Jig Is Up" became popular.

Usually, I drive west on Broad to get to my parents' home; but since I had been away from Charleston for so many months, I said to my wife, "Let's toot the boul," which is to say, let's drive around the boulevard, the southern end of the peninsula where the Ashley and Cooper Rivers meet to form the Atlantic Ocean. This boulevard is commonly known as the battery and pronounced that way in spite of the fact that those up-country provincials accuse us of calling it the "bottry."

My wife agreed, though she never is quite as enthusiastic as I am about tooting the boul. To me the battery is more than a pretty place to watch the sun set over the water. It's the place where my old colored nurse used to take her "Little Boy Blue" — a name I gave myself thinking not of Mother Goose but of the little boy in Eugene Field's poem — to play on the cannons, there in the park, maybe even on the one that started the war. The battery is the place where they had sunrise services every Easter and, about azalea time every spring, held a contest to see which of the city's Negro fish and vegetable criers was the best. Those bent and tired-looking men and women would push their carts along the sidewalk and chant:

> Lady get your dishpan,
> yhere come de schwump man,
> ra-a-a-a-a-a-a-a-aw SCHWUMP,
> schwumpee raw.

Or something on that order. White Charleston would turn out to watch — and smile. This was the place where we, when we were thirteen and devilish, would shine flashlights into parked cars at the lovers, when we were seventeen and suave, would be inside those parked cars.

Driving around the battery, I usually look at the water rather than at the front row of houses owned by the very rich, many of whom are Jewish. It's not exactly that I'm jealous of all that display of wealth, but the water is ocean water, salt water, water that goes out twice a day taking all the city sewerage with it, and then comes back in — fresh, renewed, turbulent! My grandfather told the story of an old Charleston "darky" who somehow got transplanted to upstate Carolina and one day, despairingly looking out over one of those rivers red from clay, said, "I sho' wish I was home, cause up here dere ain' no mullet in de creek, no baa'nacle on de rock, and he always ebb tide. Praise de Lawd for the flood tide."

On the west end of the battery is the Coast Guard base, where I spent many a dull Sunday as an officer in the reserves, trying to get the government to send me a certain form on which I could order certain items. "But you are supposed to have that form," they wrote back two months later. "But I don't." "But" — two months after that —"you should and besides you are not using the correct letter procedure to order that order form." And so forth. I drove by that place quickly, blinking, and then, leaving the battery, drove by the "horse lot," where the city kept its horses long ago, where we played football fifteen years ago.

Once again we were on Broad Street, the west end, riding by the block-square Colonial Lake. A Negro boy will drown every now and then in this lake, not because he was pushed in but because he doesn't know how to swim and he doesn't know that he can't swim; and it's such a pretty lake.

Driving eastward on Broad, you eventually come to my street — my street — there's something grand about its being mine. It was here that I was raised; and after my life's work is over — wherever it takes me — it is here on this street that I hope to die. My street! The elementary school that I attended is on this street, only one block north of Broad. My parents would laugh a block away when they heard me loudly singing my way home from school; grumpy people on the wrong side of Broad, irritated at the noise, would poke their heads out of second-story windows and would not laugh, but it didn't matter so much about them.

My street was the place and my late elementary school years were the time of my golden age. It was then that my friends came over to see me most every afternoon. In the big oak tree in our backyard, we had a clubhouse built on the limbs that overhung another yard. One day when we collected together to pour boiling tar on each other and play Prince of the Foxes, we found, much to our dismay, that the neighbor in the next yard, afraid that we might fall out of the tree and sue him, had cut down all the limbs on which our house was built. Immediately, we went home, got our BB guns and killed his pet squirrel to get even for that travesty of justice.

It was also my street on which the Sceeree Route began. The gang of boys a year or two older than we were first discovered this passage on which you could walk atop brick walls separating peoples' yards, all the way from Broad Street to the Battery, coming down only to cross the two intervening streets. Actually, the name Sceeree was a corruption of the name Scheewee. There was a danger that you might be turned in to the police for trespassing, a danger that you might cut yourself, as I once did — ten stitches in the knee, the most in the crowd — when you ran along Broken Bottle Wall that had pieces of glass embedded in its top to keep early-nineteenth-century thieves and bad boys from climbing over it, a danger that you might fall off those high walls at any moment. It was because of these irresistible dangers and others that the route was named Sceeree. The older boys had named it Scheewee because they'd save up all day; and, when they came to key points along it, they would scheewee.

On beginning high school, my friends climbed down from

the trees and the walls, leaving me behind. For the first time, I found myself without friends. I think the switch in my popularity, the end of my golden age, began when I backed down from an important fight — disgracing myself in my own eyes if not in the eyes of my friends, who were there and watched it all. After a couple of miserable years, first no friends, then no friends and no trees either, I was relieved when my parents decided to send me to prep school in North Carolina. There I began questioning, tentatively, not only the institution of segregation but also Charleston itself — the way one questions the divinity of Christ. Could it be that the world was bigger than my street, my crowd, my city? Was that pluff mud smell really the perfume of heaven? Could Charleston be wrong about those Nigras who live uptown and come down to our part of the city to take care of children and sell shrimp? Could they be real people — you know, like me? Just like me. I've been out of high school for ten years, and I'm still asking those questions. And this brings me to where I left off when my wife woke up the first time — asking questions.

"Well, here we are, home sweet home," I said, pulling up to the curb in front of my parents' wood frame house, with the porch on the side, in the characteristic Charleston fashion.

"Yes, and good luck," she answered, half joking, half deadly serious.

Most of the rest of what you read in this diary, I wrote day by day during the summer. I have polished it up since that time, dividing it into sections, expanding in a few places, adding most of this chapter. A friend of mine once told me that you cannot be objective about a thought until you express it; and I knew that when I faced the two Charleston worlds, objectivity was what I would need. So in this diary I express all sorts of things because I thought and felt all sorts of things. If I felt like cursing, I cursed. If I felt religious, I tried to convey that. If at times I sound like a zealous young liberal, well, I am. If at other times I sound like a segregationist, there's still much of that left in me too. If my diary is not consistent, it is because my summer was not consistent.

II

Charleston White
and Charleston Black

So it was my first experience in Charleston "society" that I thought of while I floated in the water. It's good to be home, I thought. And then, coming out of the water onto the beach, I noticed that of all the bathers not one was Negro. Theoretically, they can swim at the beach now, but, as someone has told me, "They don't go to the beach because they know they aren't wanted there." A dagger of guilt ran through me. I realized right then, at that moment, that I didn't want them on this beach either, not this beach.

Whether it be in a family Bible, the memory of a cocktail party, or here at the white beach, the black man reappears.

◗

Were you there when they crucified my Lord?
Were you there when they crucified my Lord?
Oh! Sometimes it causes me to tremble, tremble, tremble.
Were you there when they crucified my Lord?

Were you there when they nailed him to the tree?
Were you there when they nailed him to the tree?
Oh! Sometimes it causes me to tremble, tremble, tremble.
Were you there when they nailed him to the tree?

Were you there when they laid him in the tomb?
Were you there when they laid him in the tomb?
Oh! Sometimes it causes me to tremble, tremble, tremble.
Were you there when they laid him in the tomb?

— Negro Spiritual

JUNE 11. Day after tomorrow, I start my summer's work at St. Paul's Episcopal Mission Center. Late yesterday afternoon, my wife and I arrived here from Virginia and moved in with my parents. Right away we faced a major problem. The folks wanted to put us next to them in the guest bedroom, which my mother had gone to great trouble to fix up for us; but we wanted to stay in the back room, currently the junk room, because it provides some degree of privacy.

I didn't tell my wife, but I have another reason for wanting to stay there — the back room is my old room, the one I grew up in. In the days before it was painted, I would lie there in bed in the early morning and try to make animals out of the strange shapes that the watermarks had made on the plaster. After it was painted, I took great pride in that room and fixed it up nicely. I tacked three oval pictures of bearded ancestors on the wall above my desk. Then I drove a large nail in the brittle plaster above my bed, on which I hung a confederate sword. Gradually, I accumulated all sorts of things. My grandfather gave me what became my favorite decoration — a hawk's claw. He had cured it with salt and fixed it so that you could pull strings and make the claw open and close. On the night when he gave it to me, I tied the claw to a window shade cord so that when my mother came to tuck me in and, as she always did, pull down the shade, she'd scream. She did, so I left the claw dangling there permanently, that is, until a friend of mine traded me some old stamps for it. He sat behind this girl in class who had an extra large rump which enticingly overhung her chair, and with the hawk's claw being able to open and close and all, well, he figured he'd have some fun. He did, so an angry teacher confiscated it. The hawk's claw was thrown out, but most everything else I strung up or set down in my room stayed right there. In the years that I was in prep school and college, the rest of the family added their junk to mine.

Now in order for us to win the argument with my parents and move into the back room, I figured I'd have to prove that it was habitable. Thus, I spent the afternoon getting rid of the junk. Throwing the stuff out, I felt as though I was hacking at the umbilical cord that connected me with the past. Out went those three bearded ancestors with their funny black ties and their scowling faces. Out went all my high school and college notes that I had so carefully taken, carefully saved, and never looked at again. Out went clothes that were too small for me fifteen years ago, including the red football jersey, number ninety-nine, from the days of our championship "mite" team. Out went those stamps that I had gotten for the hawk's claw, along with a thousand other stamps, equally worthless. After getting rid of my junk, I started on the things the others had brought into my room. I threw out my Aunt Susie's chemistry books and her debutante dress (one of those with a large hoopskirt), a pile of correspondence between two distant cousins of mine, long dead, several old Bibles, the kind with four-leaf clovers pressed into the Book of

Exodus and a lock of your great-great-great-grandmother's hair, clipped off on her wedding day, pressed into the poem on charity in First Corinthians. From one of those Bibles a newspaper article, brown with age, about some social event, fell to the floor. On the back of it was an advertisement for a slave auction.

I managed to take several armfuls of junk out to the trash can in the yard without being seen, but on about the fourth load my mother caught me. I froze in my tracks. In a rage, she promptly summoned my sister, who lives four blocks away, and the two of them hurried out to the trash can, re-sorted the junk, and brought most of it back to the back room to be re-stored. But I stood firm. I wouldn't have it. That's my room. That's where we are going to stay — and without the junk. Either those dusty things out of the past go, or we go. Finally Mother and Sis backed down, probably because we had just returned after being away for two years. Our first victory had been won. The past had given way to social progress.

The real battle will begin Monday when I go to the Negro mission center to work under a Negro priest. God alone knows what will happen this summer. My parents and old friends at night and the Negroes at the mission during the day. How will I live in these two worlds? Will I identify primarily with my night world, or with my day world? Or will I try to find a middle position between them? I say I want social progress. But whom do I want to change? Myself? Or just other people? Already, I find myself in a contradiction. I am the one who wants to get rid of my family's junk, but I am also the one who wants to sleep in my childhood room. My wife recognizes this contradiction in me. "I can understand why you want to get involved in the racial struggle," she said, "but why *must* you choose Charleston as the place where you become involved?" I can't quite answer that yet.

Nor can I satisfactorily answer the question of one of our neighbors, an elderly and friendly sort of person. "William," he said, "how come you are going to be with the Nigras this summer?" My parents have said little to me about my work. My father did tell me that he wants me to keep my black friends out of his home. I will respect that; but what, I asked, if one comes anyway? Mother interrupted, "Your father always behaves like a gentleman in his home and there will be no trouble this summer." I hope she's right. I like change; I don't like trouble.

As my two worlds become more closely defined, and as I fight off irate parents and Charleston conservatives who shout traitor at me, and run from civil rights workers and Negroes who shout phony and do-gooder at me, I think, being a man of God anyway, I will try to follow the wisdom of my great-aunt's colored maid, Emma. Aunt Martha had been very carefully going over with Emma the ten things she should do in case of an atom bomb attack. As my aunt explained each, she noticed that Emma's eyes were getting bigger and bigger. When she finished, she said, "Now tell me, Emma, what are you going to do when you hear that siren?" "Well, I tell you, Miss Martha, when I hears that siren, I'se goin' to fall on my knees, I'se goin' to roll my eyes to me Jesus, and open me haart to she."

June 12. Today is Sunday, and we should have gone to church, me being a seminarian and all that. But I knew if I went to church, I'd be asked what I was doing this summer;

and I didn't feel like getting into that, not today. Instead, my wife and I went to the beach so that we could lie out in the sun, swim in the surf, and get away from my obsession with the racial conflict for at least a little while.

Along the South Carolina coast, there are a number of islands that are deserted, windswept, and sandy; but the one we went to today is fully populated with summer residents. While my wife lies on the beach, I usually float in the water beyond the breakers and imagine that I am in the middle of the ocean having escaped from an enemy ship in which I was a prisoner. Then, after I exhaust that story, I think about other things. Today it was my first debutante party, which was held years ago in one of those front row beach houses that I could see from where I was floating.

Up until recently Charleston people migrated to the beaches every summer to get away from the oppressive heat. My friends and I would visit often in those places. Now, with all the air-conditioning, the Charleston people can enjoy the coolness of the beach right at home — without ever leaving their beloved city. They have either sold or rented their houses to upstate people who must not be so satisfied with their home towns. I well remember the summer bridge games, the hot-dog roasts on the beach, the dances on the patios. But most of all I remember that debutante party.

Ordinarily, all the debutante parties are held during Christmas vacation, but that particular year, the summer after my senior year in high school, there were so many parties scheduled for the ten or twelve days at Christmas that some of the smaller ones had to be held during the summertime. Not only does each girl have her own ball or ball-size reception, but she also has a number of cocktail parties, suppers, breakfasts,

brunches, and lunches given for her, the number depending
on how popular her parents are and on how many parties her
parents have given for other debutantes in the past. The
Christmas that my crowd of boys was on "the list," we were
invited to fifty-six parties. We made most of them, we managed to go on five or six duck hunts, and we were able to stag-
ger to the midnight Christmas service at St. Tom's. The
ironic thing about these parties is that the girls are supposed to
be meeting new people as they make their "bow" to society,
but they end up spending the whole time, the whole crazy fifty-
six parties, with boys they've known all their lives. When a
Charleston girl finishes making her debut, she is so sick of
Charleston boys that she'll generally marry someone from out
of town or someone a half-generation older than she is, or
she'll move to New York and look for a job.

But I'm getting ahead of my story, which is about my first
encounter with the debutantes that particular summer, at that
same house up there on the beach. The party was given for a
girl named Nora. My date, Antoinette, was one of the girls I
had grown up with. Father called me aside earlier on the day
of the party and told me that they would be serving mixed
drinks at the party and I could have one, but no more, "because, William, you don't know how to drink." Antoinette's
father had given her the same warning. We chuckled as we
compared notes and agreed to show those "old buzzards" a
thing or two.

At the party, there were a few young people but mostly there
were adults standing around drinking and talking about, as
well as I could tell, other parties — and with great dignity
too. "Oh no," Antoinette said, "this isn't going to be a fun
party." We were introduced to the guests as "Mr." and

"Miss." I punched Antoinette to make her laugh at this new title, but she stood just as solemn as I.

I got us drinks from the colored bartender — gin and tonic, I thought that sounded good. We drank those in a hurry and agreed that they were too bitter. So on the next round, I asked Arthur to give us each a Scotch on rye; they were even worse. Someone said something about the frozen daiquiris being "out of this world." "Arthur, old man," I said, "two double frozen daiquiris." We liked those so much we kept going back for more — a good man that Arthur. I don't know whether the party was beginning to loosen up or whether the change was solely subjective, but Antoinette and I were suddenly having a grand time. Nora's nickname being "No-no," Antoinette went over, slapped her mother's back and told her that this was a lovely no-no she was having. I was showing off in the young peoples' corner, chugalugging sherry.

When it came time for us to leave, we told everyone in the place how much we had enjoyed the no-no, and on the way out we fell into an oleander bush.

Suddenly, I was sick. I ran for one of those sand dunes up there. And that's all I remember. Some friends got me home and into bed without my parents seeing me.

Breakfast conversation with Father the next morning went something like this:

"Well, Son, how was the party last night?"

"Fine, Father, just fine."

"Who'd you meet?"

"Oh, lots of people. . . . Well, I met Nora's parents."

"Sure you met them, who else?"

"Oh yes, Father, I met Arthur, the bartender. He's a good old colored fellow isn't he?"

"Yes, Son, one of the few old-timey ones left. He was tending bar when I was coming along. Did you tell him who you were?"

"Yes sir, he remembered you." I was sick inside, the little breakfast I'd eaten had made me even sicker, but the fact that I seemed to be getting away with my drinking bout the night before was encouraging me, giving me new life. While Father talked on about Arthur, I thanked the Lord that I had remembered him. He was, in fact, the only one from the party that I could remember. All the rest of the faces were vague and shadowy. Only the colorful, laughing face of Arthur stood out. But, at the moment, I thought I had the victory won. . . .

"Have some more eggs, Son."

"I don't believe I care for any, Father."

"But you always take seconds."

"Not today, thank you." I was about ready to run to the sand dunes again.

"Son! You didn't drink too much last night did you. . . ." And so forth. I hadn't fooled anyone after all. While he lectured me, I felt ashamed and sick and wondered how I could ever face any of those people or my family again, and guilty and hated myself. When Father said that I probably wouldn't be invited to any more debutante parties — ever — I only hoped he was right.

So it was my first experience in Charleston "society" that I thought of while I floated in the water. In spite of the fiasco of that night, I was content and happy with that memory. It's funny how even a bad memory of Charleston often becomes a good one, one you enjoy recalling. It's good to be home, I thought. And then, coming out of the water onto the beach, I noticed that of all the bathers not one was Negro. Theoretically, they can swim at the beach now, but as someone has told me, "They don't go to the beach because they know they aren't wanted there." A dagger of guilt ran through me. I realized right then, at that moment, that I didn't want them on this beach either, not this beach.

Whether it be in a family Bible, the memory of a cocktail party, or here at the white beach, the black man reappears. The Negro, the suppressed Negro, seems to pop out at you when you least expect him.

June 13. St. Paul's Mission Center, really more of a community center than anything else, is a converted Episcopal church, one of those that was built a long time ago in a white middle-class neighborhood that has long since become one of the worst Negro slums in town. There are still a good many graves around the church, some of which are kept up by the descendents of the white folks who are buried there. If the graves could be moved, the kids would have a much larger space to play in. But there is a good argument for keeping the graves there. The stones make excellent obstacles for games of follow-the-leader and barricades for cowboys and Indians.

The porch of the building, about four feet above the ground, evidently serves as the place where things are painted. It is streaked and smeared with as many colors as there were in Joseph's coat. Holding up the roof of the porch are four large columns, which are pure white above the reach of the tallest child, dirt brown below. On one column there is drawn with a black crayon two smiling faces and two attempts to spell a certain four-letter word, one "tird," one "trid."

Inside the building there is a large room, once the nave of

the church. Two offices have been built near the doorway. Overhead, the choir balcony has been converted into a library and an all-purpose room. High on the wall on the opposite side of the room, there are tacked up in great red letters, cut out of cardboard, the words GOOD MANNERS, not "God is love" or "Jesus saves," but something of a more immediate concern. The condition of this large room explains why good manners are so stressed. In the middle of the floor there is a pool table with broken chairs flung across the felt. Lying on the floor are the pool cues, along with Batman cards, pieces of Coke bottles, checkers, marbles, broken croquet mallets, torn baseball mitts, and gloves. In one corner there is a large bookcase, which is only about half full. The rest of the books and the magazines are on the floor nearby. In another corner there is a dust-covered electric stove, which probably hasn't worked in years. A number of the stained glass windows of the old church have been broken out.

On the other side of the nave are several classrooms, the chapel, and the two bathrooms. There is not one dirty or profane word written on the walls of the men's room. How strange it is — we white people rebel in secret by writing "Fuck you" on hidden bathroom walls; these Negroes rebel in the open, saying the same thing by tearing up their own mission center.

I arrived at St. Paul's about eight-thirty, before anyone else had come, except for two young men who were outside in the graveyard burning trash in one of those rusty barrels. I walked over and introduced myself. They were very pleasant. One of them, Adam, tells me he's the caretaker and odd-jobs man and has been working at the center, with a few interruptions, since it opened four years ago. Adam and I think we met each other once before. I worked at this same center three years ago on Sunday afternoons for two or three months. While Adam doesn't normally work on Sundays, it was probably then that we met. In this city, where else could we have met? The other man is named Mike.

Adam had to go inside to do some work, but Mike and I stayed outside and chatted awhile, poking the fire. He says he dropped out of school here in Charleston in the eleventh grade and went to New York seeking a job. After a year and a half of Harlem, he decided that the big city was too big for him. So he returned and hasn't been doing much of anything since Christmas. He hopes to join the Job Corps, and it is that item of business that brings him to the center today. Mike says he really wants to learn a trade this time. Though he is only twenty, he's already kicking himself for not finishing high school.

I asked Mike a lot of questions about the center, some of which he could answer. Up until now, no one has told me exactly what the center does. When I worked here before, Father Andrews was just getting the place started and wasn't here much on Sundays. He wrote me last spring telling me that he would be glad to have me work as an assistant for him this summer, but he did not give me any idea of what I would be doing. The question which I have not asked him and will not, the big question for me is: Will I be expected to participate in civil rights demonstrations? I quiver inside at the thought of demonstrating, and at the thought of refusing to demonstrate on an issue that I may be much in sympathy with. But I may be just imagining a problem. After all, I have never heard of Father Andrews's being involved in the few sit-ins and the marches we've had in Charleston.

Starting with Mike's description and filling in with comments from others around, I have determined that the center does at least this much. First, it participates in three government anti-poverty programs: it has a Head Start program for about thirty kindergarten-age children; it acts as the Job Corps recruiting agency for Charleston County; it trains two or three high school dropouts at a time from the Neighborhood Youth Corps. Let me note in passing that I had no idea these government programs were operational in Charleston. Do they not get proper news coverage locally? or, do the people I know just not bother to read and learn about them? Second, the center serves as a playground for young children in an effort to get them off the street and as a meeting place for older boys who come to play cards and Ping-Pong. Third, it provides some sort of spiritual leadership for the community though it apparently makes no attempt to proselytize. Most of the kids who come here are Baptists, Jehovah's Witnesses, and African-Methodist-Episcopalians. No one seems to know exactly when services are held. They grin when I ask them as though that may be up to me.

About nine o'clock, the rest of the staff began arriving. First, Linda — the white girl, about twenty-five, who's in the employ of the church in the capacity of Father Andrews' chief assistant and of the government in the capacity of Job Corps recruiter. She's a South Carolina girl, short like my wife, and quite blond. Her office is barely large enough for a desk and the chair on which I sat. Linda and I talked for about an hour. You'd think we would have talked about integration, major social problems, demonstrations, the big things; but no, we talked about the number of Job Corps recruits, the number of Ping-Pong balls on hand, the Bible School, which starts tomorrow and which, she thinks, I'll be working with. I'd like to know what Linda's motives were in picking a Negro slum mission in her home state to work in. Could they be the same as mine? I suspect that whatever her motives were when she started, her primary concern now is to get the job done, you know, like any other job. Linda's whole life seems to be devoted to her work.

Then Mrs. Wilson — the middle-aged Negro woman, who, Linda tells me, is known for telling Bible stories and who along with Adam is a mainstay of the center. She is currently in charge of the Head Start program and is, besides, a great power in the community. Adam told me later in the day to stay on the good side of her. Once she got angry with the government office that oversees the center over some bureaucratic matter and "put the bad mouth" on them. The next day the Head Start class dropped from thirty to four.

Then, two white girls — the high school dropouts in the N.Y.C. I think they wash dishes and do things like that during the day. And finally, the three teachers in the Head Start program — one white, two Negro. All of the staff was friendly, though only Linda and Adam had known I was coming to work here this summer.

About nine-thirty, the kids began arriving en masse, from three years old to twenty, some waiting around for kindergarten, some waiting around to see if Father Andrews knew of any summer jobs, some just waiting around; some very carefully dressed, some in ragged hand-me-downs. I noticed one little boy, the blackest one there, fighting off his six- and seven-year-old friends who were surrounding him and chanting, "Black-y-mo, Black-y-mo, Ho! Ho! Ho! Black-y-mo." I think this name is a version of "blackamoor" but am not positive.

Father Andrews didn't arrive until eleven-thirty. I would guess he's about forty. I remember his telling me when I worked at the center before that he had a master's degree in political science as well as his seminary degree. He's a nice-looking man with a kind and sensitive face. When he came walking briskly in, I jumped out of the corner where I had been trying to stay out of the way, went over and greeted him. "Father Andrews," I said, "I'm ready to work. I'm tired of studying and going to church. I'm ready to get down to business in the world. So just put me to work."

"Fine, William," he said. "You spend the next few days observing what's going on and organizing the Bible School, which will begin tomorrow and run for the next two weeks." Then, "Now if you'll excuse me, I have got to make some phone calls. I'll go over your job with you in more detail later on this afternoon." He never did get a chance to give me any more instructions. But I did what he told me. I observed by playing Ping-Pong with some of the older boys and I began organizing the Bible School by signing up most of the kids who were hanging around the center. Mrs. Wilson told me what to do. You write down their names, addresses, ages, and their mothers' names. Fathers seem to be scarce. As one of the little boys expressed it, "Timothy dere, *he* got a pa."

Late in the afternoon, I found myself talking with one of the teachers — the white one, Sally. About Linda's age, she is also from South Carolina. She's tall and holds her head high. During the school year, she teaches English at a white high school. This is her second summer as a teacher in the Head Start program, her first summer at St. Paul's. Since Mrs. Wilson and another one of the teachers will be away for most of the summer to receive training, Sally tells me that she will be in charge of Head Start here at the center. "What made you decide to do this kind of work?" I asked. She couldn't tell me, other than to say that this was a good summer job for a teacher. She was quick to point out, however, that it was not political liberalism that brought her here, for she is, she says, a conservative.

In a way I hope Sally is a conservative, as she says she is, though I wonder about that. This whole region prides itself on conservatism, each person trying to outdo the other. The only way *they* will ever take the initiative in trying to alleviate the conditions of the suppressed Negro is if a conservative leads them, a person who is one *of* them. Linda and I are from them but probably no longer of them.

June 14. This morning we began the Bible School. Since no one told me what to do, I went ahead and organized it myself on the basis of the educational material that the diocese had sent. About forty children showed up for it. We began with the suggested worship service, which I think is too dry for these folks, though they did seem to listen, whether because they are naturally attentive in church or because they don't know exactly what to make of a white preacher, I don't know. As I looked out over the congregation, I gulped twice, once because I've never been in a room with so many black people before, once because I'm brand new at conducting worship services. At seminary, I've studied Bible and Paul Tillich's theology for the last two years, but I haven't had much practical experience.

After the service, we broke up into three classes. Father Andrews's wife took one, a girl about sixteen took one, and I took the older kids, those nine to fourteen years old. The curriculum for the two weeks' period is the Ten Commandments. Today, we talked about the first one. By their questions and answers, they demonstrated that they have had some sort of religious training in their own churches. Moreover, I'm already impressed by their religious response. As one girl said, "When the spirit hit you, you can't let him go."

Following the class, we had our handicraft period. I neatly laid out on the table the paint, the brushes, and the paper. They calmly waited until I had finished. And then. . . . Have you ever seen a bunch of wild Indians preparing for the war path? Have you ever seen a green Bible School teacher painted blue, and red, and even greener? After that mess, we had our outdoor recreation, which was more fun, for me anyway. We closed Bible School with lunch, consisting of rice and okra made into gumbo, a favorite dish among both races in Charleston. The fact that I was given only a spoon to eat it with didn't matter.

It was for the meal that Richard, short and stout, appeared. He is, the fellows tell me, eleven years old. Some say he's "deef," some say he's retarded, some say both; but everyone knows him. He seems to divide his time between roaming the neighborhood and chasing after street sweepers. Richard sat next to me for lunch. I didn't mind the dirt caked on his clothes and on his hands, I could even put up with the body odor; but when he smiled, showing me his badly decayed teeth, I couldn't finish my gumbo, good as it was. I can see I have a long way to go. For some reason, however, Richard took a liking to me and followed me around all day.

Lunch was over. My Bible School duties had ended. Father Andrews still hadn't told me any more about my job. I could see him through the window of his office, sitting at his desk, doing some paper work, completely oblivious to the fact that I was at the center. His ignoring me made me uneasy, particularly because I had no idea what to do with myself. Should I stay out of everyone's way, or should I become involved somehow? There is, however, one thing worse than no job description, and that is, a regimented job description, the kind that you find in the government. At least this way, I'll be able to poke around.

About three in the afternoon, the Ping-Pong and pool group, guys between sixteen and twenty, began showing up. These are the fellows who are just waiting around. I waited around with them all afternoon. Doing nothing is catching. I had begun the afternoon planning to start some youth activities but ended up doing nothing, playing Ping-Pong — losing all but one game — and swapping gibes with one fellow, about eighteen, who calls himself "King" or "The Greatest." I got the impression that this group of young men had spent their whole life in the mission center neighborhood and had spent it waiting around together. Their range of conversation seemed to be limited to the games they were playing and to the discussion of a few girls, the mention of whose names evoked telling grins. For a while, I was conscious of being bored; but then I seemed to drift into the mood of somnolence, talking about Ping-Pong, pool, saying the hell with it all.

Later in the afternoon, Adam and I struck up a conversation. I asked him what the seminarian who worked at the center last summer had done with his time. The thing that Adam remembered most favorably was the "staff meetings." Every afternoon this seminarian, himself white, and Adam would walk down to the corner grocery store, Mr. Dick's, and have a beer. Adam laughed and added, "We'd do that just before the afternoon worship service." "Adam," I said, "we aren't going to have a worship service this afternoon, but let's go down to the corner. I'll buy you a beer anyway." He thought that was a fine idea.

Mr. Dick's is run by white people — they were friendly to Adam but had nothing to say to me — and serves this Negro section of town. There were big signs in the windows advertising chicken necks and beef kidneys. The beer was only cool, I guess because Mr. Dick wants to save on electricity; but our staff meeting was most helpful. Adam told me about the power structure at the center — both among the staff and among the older boys. When I asked him about Father Andrews, he said, "Father Andrews confirmed me," but nothing else. Adam told me that the group — he meant the Ping-Pong group — liked me. And he agreed to let me know how I was doing as the summer progressed. After the beer, I felt much less sleepy, much more enthusiastic about organizing some sort of youth activities. The place desperately needs organization. Not only is there nothing at all planned for many of the kids, there is also very little co-ordination among the various programs at the center. Adam, for example, is paid by church and state and doesn't know who his chief is, so he spends a lot of time "slacking off." Even the Bible School seems poorly organized. No one at the center but me has a watch; and no one but me was ready to start the worship service on time. Adam laughed at my concern over promptness but seemed pleased that I am enthusiastic about trying to organize.

On the way back to the center, I noticed for the first time that Adam has a short beard that forms a point just under his chin. Also, he's not as big as I had first thought. Though he's about my height, five-ten, I'll bet he's only twenty-six or twenty-eight inches around the waist. If Adam had lived two generations ago, he'd have been described as a good and loyal nigger by the white Charleston people. As I waved good-bye to him and got in my car to go home, I could not help but wonder what new relationship, if any, will develop between Adam and those people? What sort of chance will a good man like him have in his lifetime?

June 15. Today I was determined to have a hymn during the worship service, but I could not lead it for I have no voice (even my seminary brothers move away from me in chapel), nor could I find anyone else to lead it, among either the teachers or the regular staff. I'm told that Father Andrews has a good voice, but he doesn't come in until later in the morning, and I'd probably be afraid to ask him anyway. The hymn that I asked them to lead was: "Were you there when they crucified my Lord?" It is the only Negro spiritual in my church's hymnal. Just when I was about to give up, this deep, booming voice made its way from the kitchen to the other side of the nave, shaking the pots and pans:

> O-o-o-o-o-o-o-o-o-o-h, sometimes it causes me to
> Trembo   Trembo   Trembo
> Were you there when they crucified my Lord?

Mrs. Martin who reminds me of the gentle person who helped raise me — the gentle person I wasn't allowed to kiss good night — was the one I was looking for. She proudly led the hymn and it went very well. Most of the children seemed to know it.

On beginning the third verse, I looked up from the hymnal at my congregation, forty children, many in rags, stuffed into a room no larger than the back of one of those ancient trucks that haul cotton and tomato pickers around, a room with several years of greasy hand prints on the walls, children who have nothing, neither toys nor affection, children who are being crushed by the weight of a society they do not even comprehend. They are the dregs of humanity, an aristocrat once told me, the bottom. A room that stinks of unwashed and sweaty bodies, children who know about freezing cold in the winter and who have no beach to go to in the summer, little children who know about suffering and death, sickness without sympathy, a room of children singing loudly, triumphantly, and appreciating fully the hymn that I love but mostly in a sentimental way, the hymn that I've found myself singing all day long. These children know what it's like to be there while society, a far-off "they" to them that lives on the other side of town, crucifies our Lord.

In the Bible class, we were talking about the Second Commandment, "Thou shalt not make to thyself any 'gravy' images," when it occurred to me that now might be a good time to talk about what the true God is like. I asked the group — four more students today — how they would draw God.

"I'd draw him pure white with long yellow curls," Cathy answered as she looked up to the ceiling of the library room trying to picture God.

"You'd draw him white?" I asked. "Why white?"

" 'Cause he just as pure as white," responded black Andrew.

"Das right, das right." Several children were joining in.

"How many," I asked, "think God is black?" No response.

"Well, how many think he's brown?" I was becoming a little impatient.

One boy raised his hand and said confidently, "He brown."

"Why's he brown?"

"*I* brown, aynor?" ("Aynor" is a contraction of "ain't" and "it" and is roughly equivalent to *n'est-ce pas.*)

"How many agree with Jerome" — whose other names are Ronnie and Lip — "that God is brown?"

As I looked hopefully around the room to see if anyone else would raise his hand — none did — I was trying to remember my theology and at the same time put it in their terms. God, defined not as the Infinite, but as the highest symbol that finite man can conceive of, must be the subjective projection of the individual person, for only then can he be a fully personal and fully living God. This came out, "You are black, or brown; I'm white. Your God is your color, Jerome is right, my God is my color. But he's the same God."

The kids began snickering in an embarrassed way when I compared their skin color to mine, so I thought I would change the subject. Besides, I was getting myself into one of those hopeless religious paradoxes that theologians are always trying to make sense of. How can God be fully black and fully white and still be the same God?

But I *will* come back to God's color another day, for I am determined that they learn to color God correctly as they picture him in their imaginative minds. Tillich said that the religious symbol is "double-edged." It brings the infinite God down to the symbol used for God. At the same time, it elevates the finite thing used as the symbol. For example, when we speak of God the Father, we not only bring the Infinite down to the human institution of fatherhood, but we also make holy the human institution of fatherhood itself. A ten-year-old Negro does not know it, but when he makes God white, he is elevating and making holy white skin, not his own. How can he ever think of himself as equal as long as God is white and his black skin makes himself something less than holy? And if he can't think of himself as equal, how can he ever act equal to the white man?

In one sense, a Negro makes to himself a graven image when he makes God black — that's part of the predicament of sinful, finite man, every human concept of the Infinite being a false one. But if the Negro makes God white, not only does he make a graven image, but he also makes a God who is not truly *his* God, a God who is not fully personal, a God who will keep him from being a full person. A God who eventually will die in his mind and who eventually will cause him to die as a man. When the infinite dimension of the symbol dies the finite dimension dies too.

These kids can teach me about the crucifying of our Lord and the pathos involved in that. I must teach them that Jesus allowed himself to be crucified so that *they* might be holy.

June 16. The Bible School continues to absorb most of my interest. Yesterday afternoon, I did manage to go shopping with Linda for some recreation equipment — jump ropes, horseshoes, a basketball — but for the most part I either work on the Bible School program or I hang out with the boys around the pool table where "de livin' is easy."

This morning, I made some changes in the worship service, working mostly on the procession. I wanted all the children to march into the little chapel — two by two, as the animals marched into Noah's ark — but I needed a cross for someone to carry at the head of the line. I thought about trying to borrow one from another Episcopal church but soon realized that would be stupid. Why not, instead, use something familiar to these kids? Yes, I can make the cross relevant (that's the big word in seminaries nowadays) and avoid begging at the same time. I got two broomsticks and a coat hanger and in thirty seconds had a cross.

The broomsticks are as dirty as the hands and the faces of the children, and the cross is as makeshift as the church-converted mission center; and I was pleased with the finished product. In fact, that cross may be more like the original one than the carefully finished crosses that lead the regal parades from one side of our Episcopal churches to the other. I got the biggest devil, Andrew, ten years old ordinarily (eleven when he's trying to join the Boy Scout troop I've been thinking of starting), to carry the cross. Two others, Timothy and Isaac, carried the Episcopal Church and American flags. I lined up the kids, and we marched in with me bringing up the rear. Since our Bible School is growing, it is even harder for everyone to fit in the chapel; so we sat all over the place. We even had a couple sitting in the sanctuary. The cross and flag bearers of their own accord stood rigidly at attention throughout the service at the front of the chapel, holding the church and national standards high. I smiled as I thought how unorthodox I was being and how much I was enjoying it.

During the class that followed the worship, I had planned to discuss the Sixth Commandment, "Thou shall not kill." When this commandment is explained to Sunday School children, it is always interpreted as "killing with words." You want to make the commandment relevant, and what Sunday

School kid is concerned with actual murder? So I worked up a nice, short talk about non-physical killing and was knocked off guard when the class told me that a man from their neighborhood was murdered in a card game the night before. Casually, I put my notes aside and let them talk for the rest of the period. Each one of them gave me a different version of what happened. All were anxious to talk about it. One boy, who said his brother witnessed the killing, told us that Mr. Charlie was "dozin'" (teasing) his opponent in a card game. His opponent lost his temper, pulled out a pistol, and shot him right between the eyes. Rather than talk about whether or not you should say bad things to other kids, we ended up talking about whether or not you should carry knives and guns.

After the class, I took the Bible School boys down to the corner lot to play baseball (there's not enough room in the mission yard — too many graves in the way). It took some work, but I finally got them organized into two teams. I laughed when the first boy to get a hit, Sneed, a bright boy about twelve years old, ran to third base instead of first. No one tried to stop him. Can you imagine that, a red-blooded American boy, one we may be sending to war in a few years, not knowing the simplest rules of baseball! I laughed, but I could have cried.

Once the boys got the swing of it, they loved the game. We were playing with one of those plastic bats and balls, and you'd have thought it was the Yankees playing the Dodgers. I shouted at them, laughed with them, refereed for them, and didn't give a damn what those white people thought, the ones who were looking at us curiously as they passed by the lot.

The mission center kids seem to need organization as much as anything else. Even in the ball game they could not play without my close supervision. When I left my post behind the catcher for a few minutes, they began arguing over who would bat next and would have wrecked the game if I had not returned to make peace.

After a long day, the beer tasted mighty good. Adam bought it today.

Since I wrote the above, a close friend of ours has come over for a visit and a couple of drinks. Last spring this fellow offered to coach boxing in his free time. Our conversation went like this:

"Brian, I sure am glad you came over. I've been wanting to talk to you about the center. It's great that you're going to do some volunteer work there. Boxing is exactly the sort of activity these boys need. It will give them a chance to express themselves, to learn some discipline."

"Yes, well, I do still want to work with you there, but several things have come up. Maybe in two or three weeks I'll be free enough to do some coaching. How much time do you think it'll take?"

"About three hours a week. What's the matter? Last spring when I talked to you you were enthusiastic about this. Now you sound like it's going to be a chore, or am I hearing you wrong?"

"It's not that so much. I don't regard coaching them as a chore, but maybe I'm *not* as enthusiastic."

"Why?"

"I'll tell you why. I don't want it to get out around town that I'm working with Negroes."

"You weren't worried about that last spring. What's happened?"

"Well, I made the mistake of telling a few people what I planned to do, and they . . ."

"Who?"

"Now calm down, Barnwell. That's none of your business. But I will tell you this, they thought I was crazy, insane, to coach Negroes. One of them, a man who works at the Y.M.C.A. — which by the way is not integrated — thought I was joking. I never did convince him, and it's probably a good thing that he didn't believe me. He's one of those red-neck types and . . ."

"My God, Brian, how could any rational person, red-neck, high society, or otherwise, object to this sort of work. This isn't the organized civil rights movement, you know. It's just an attempt to meet a need, a very obvious need of the people of our city. They do look on the Negroes as people, don't they?"

"Oh, I suppose some of them do, but for the most part I don't think they take the Negroes seriously as people. Just as they don't seem to take integration of the schools seriously. They look at it as something temporary, something that doesn't really have much to do with them."

"You seem to be taking working with Negroes very seriously. You surprise me that you let them scare you off. I thought you were more independent than that, not being from Charleston yourself."

"You really sound like a preacher now. Look, I am independent. Remember that I spent a good bit of time in the ghetto myself after I got out of the Navy, the New York ghetto. I'm using my independence, as you call it, to become a part of Charleston, and I don't want it spoiled by word getting out that I'm working with Negroes. And you are wrong

about something else. I *am* from Charleston — originally.
My family comes from here. In fact, this is where they came
in the seventeenth century."

"Brian, it sounds to me like you've sold out. No, I won't say
that, because who am I to talk? Maybe being away from
Charleston has made me forget exactly how people feel on
race down here. I admit that when I worked at the center
before, I hated to go outside the building; I was afraid that
some stray white would pass and make fun of me. At least if
you do coach boxing, you'll be doing it in the open, not inside.
But I also admit that that fear of mine seems stupid to me
now. So stupid."

"Maybe so."

"Are you sure there is not some other reason you're reluc-
tant to work at the center?"

"Do you mean am I myself prejudiced?"

"Yes, I guess so."

"I don't think I have any strong feelings on race either way.
I'm emotionally neutral."

"Well, fellow, I'm emotional as hell about it. Maybe if you
had thrown eggs at niggers as we did when we first got our
drivers' licenses, you'd be emotional too."

"But, Barnwell, I didn't throw eggs at them. When you
were doing that I was living in Texas with my parents. They
can lead their life, I'll lead mine. I told you I'd help with the
coaching, and I suppose I will. I enjoy work with children,
black and white; but don't expect too much from me."

We continued our talk over a second drink and I told
Brian that his coolness on this race issue bothered me. I
thought he might have a healthier attitude than I since he
wasn't all torn up by guilt, but that he might be missing some-

thing too. I'm just beginning to find out what's going on in the ghetto of Charleston, our so-called beautiful and historic city, and I told him I had a strong idea that we had a potentially revolutionary situation on our hands.

"You are getting carried away with this thing, William."

"Maybe. But I get the idea that something is building up in these Negroes. Oh, on the surface, they smile and are friendly. But they sit around all day, hardly ever doing anything constructive — there's nothing constructive for them to do — and it makes me wonder what's going on inside of them. I really think we've suppressed these same people more than the Russians and French suppressed the peasants, and look at all the energy that was released when they finally revolted."

He didn't share my concern. He doubted the comparison.

As Brian and I finished off our third drink, we were becoming chummy again. He's going to think some more about whether he wants to work at the center and let me know in a week or so. If he'll just go down there a few times, I know he'll get attached to those kids and won't care about being the center of gossip. But I have to wait and see.

June 17. As soon as I got off work this evening, my wife and I went with my parents on a yacht cruise that some of their friends were having.

We had supper and drinks as we floated about the harbor watching the sun set over Charleston, watching the lights on the battery come on a few at a time, until they were the only thing visible — those lights shining in the darkness. There were about twelve people on the yacht, six conversations going on. I managed to talk to most everyone during the course of the night. Since all but three of the people on the cruise were related to me, most of the conversations were about family.

"Your great-great-uncle sailed around the world twice."

"Really?"

"Yes, he wrote home from all parts of the world. Your Aunt Hannah still has those letters. I was reading them over last week. Your great-great-uncle, my grandfather, was not only a good man but an interesting man too."

How the kids at the mission center would enjoy this cruise. Not the sunset and the beautiful old Charleston part, but a yacht, a boat! I wonder if any of them have ever been on a boat.

"Do you remember your great-great-uncle very well?"

"Do I remember, oh yes, I remember him, well, I remember him some."

"A good man he was. Did I ever tell you about the time . . ."

The kids made masks out of paper plates during the handicraft period this morning, while I looked on, curious to see how many colored their masks black or brown. As you recall, we missed out on God. There was only one brown God in the group; but today we scored a victory, eight Negro faces, three Indian faces, only two attempts to produce a white face; and of course several masks were torn up before they reached the crayon stage. If these boys and girls don't try to hide their skin colors behind a white mask, maybe there is some hope for God too.

"How do you remember your great-great-uncle?"

"I remember him as a kind old man."

But then there were conversations about my work at the center and about the Negro in Charleston. An older woman, a distant cousin of mine, Lois, whom I've always thought to be as shy and as conservative as the rest of her family, surprised me by telling me about the terrible conditions of the Negro ghetto, by telling me that we have a responsibility to do something about it. She said that she realized this when she began going to a white church in a predominantly colored area and was put in charge of locking up the recreation equipment while the colored children, their fingers clutching the wire mesh fence, looked on in envy from the outside. Why shouldn't they be allowed to use the equipment? Here she was, the one responsible for seeing that they did not use it. "William," she said, "I hope you'll stick with this kind of work, even after you finish seminary. No one is doing anything to help them, no one, not really. We have so much and we do so little. I remember back in the days of the depression how we all shared our food and looked out for each other, black and white alike, but not now. Now we only look out for ourselves."

I told her that I could be interested in doing this kind of work full time, but that it gets discouraging at times. I told her how I was encouraged by the black masks this morning but how, this afternoon, something upset me, made me feel that in the first place, I don't have any right working at the center and, that in the second place, there is nothing I can do to improve conditions there anyway. She seemed interested so I told her what happened.

Late in the afternoon, down the street from the center, there was a vicious fight between two women, one of whom had a stick. All the kids ran out to watch. Stupidly, I went along. While the two women were threatening each other, I was standing a few feet out in the street, wondering whether I should try to stop the fight, unaware that I was blocking an automobile with four Negro men in it. Suddenly those men were out of the car, screaming curses at me, shaking their fists, shouting at me to get back to where I belong. And they didn't mean back to the confines of the mission center. Nothing I could have done would have satisfied them. Nothing. It was too late.

Cousin Lois listened and then said, "Now, William, those were four men. You aren't working with them. Your job is to help those little children at the center. It's not too late. It's never too late to do the right thing."

I needed that push tonight.

Brian must have been talking to people other than those on the yacht. Though only two or three were enthusiastic about my work, all of them seemed to give at least a tacit approval, except perhaps my parents. I get the idea that they really do not like my being involved with the Negroes in any way; but as my mother says, "We are going to try not to stand in your way."

June 18. No entry.

June 19. Today is Sunday. Since talking to Cousin Lois on Friday, I feel much better about going to church at St. Thomas' and facing people who may not approve of my work. And besides, I can't stay away from my church forever.

I am the eighth generation in my family to attend St. Thomas' Church, the eighth generation to sit in a particular pew. Many of my ancestors are buried in the graveyard, some under the shadow of John C. Calhoun's tomb. When I was a boy, we played on these graves, much in the way that the St.

Paul's children play on theirs. St. Thomas' is a large church and looks very empty during a summer service when it is only about one fourth full. But it's a beautiful old church with a high ceiling, a large stained glass window above the altar, and balconies on either side and at the rear of the nave. It's in the rear balcony that they seated a group of Negroes who arrived at church one Sunday a decade or two ago. I suppose it was in the balconies and along the sides of the nave that the house slaves sat in the first part of this church's history. The only Negroes I've ever seen in the church are the sexton and the family servants who were invited to weddings and funerals and who were once or twice given seats of honor. Technically, under a recent ruling of the national Episcopal Church, every local church must seat Negroes in the same way that they seat whites. Thus, the congregation lives in dread of the day when another group of Negroes will show up. They all wonder what the minister will do. "If he lets 'em in, I'm getting out," say some. "No, why not let 'em in," say others. "Once they have *proven* that they can go to a white church, they'll be satisfied and won't want to come back." This second group of people doesn't know just how right it is about the Negro not wanting to worship with them. If I had worshiped with people like Mrs. Martin and those mission center kids all my life, I wouldn't want to return to this dull, formal service either.

I managed to pay attention to the words of the first hymn and the two Bible lessons fairly well; but when it came time for the prayers, my mind started drifting as it usually does in church. Most of the people that were here today attended that now famous parish meeting, held three or four years ago, to determine whether or not we as a local church should refuse to pay the full amount that the diocese had assessed us. Usually, the agreement to pay the assessment is a routine matter. But that year, the vestry had refused by a vote of ten or eleven to one to pay the money in an effort to protest the liberal policies of our national church, its recent statements on integration in particular. Since it is the diocese and not the local church that is assessed by the national church, the vestry voted to reduce the amount it paid to the diocese. That was the closest they could come to striking at the national church without actually withdrawing from it.

The vestry was fair enough to put their decision up to the congregation for a vote of ratification even though this procedure is not legally required. It was for this vote that the parish meeting was held. For years there has been growing in this stately old church a split between the strong conservatives and the mild conservatives, between those who want to keep the Negroes out of the church altogether and those who want to let them come in until they get tired of worshiping with the whites, between those who will tolerate no difference of opinion on race and those who are willing to talk about it. There had been many phone calls, made by people on both sides before that parish meeting.

When the night arrived, the parish hall was overflowing with Episcopalians. Not this many members of the church had come for a meeting of any kind since the previous Easter. There's one thing to be said about racial arguments in the South, they create interest. Anybody who wanted to got a chance to speak. Many of the most influential men in Charleston spoke that night, for and against, a few in the style of the nineteenth-century Southern orator, reminiscent of old Calhoun himself. When it came my turn to speak, I was terrified. Though I did manage to identify myself with the mild conservatives, I was able to say little of meaning.

One of the last men to speak shocked everyone. He represented neither camp. Emotionally charged, he stood up and said that the vestry was being beguiled by certain John Birch members in our midst, that these political rightists were using the church as a tool for their own ends and nothing more, that the very fact of that meeting showed how backward and how totally unChristian St. Thomas' Church was. And then, almost shouting, "You live in dread of integration. Do you want to see an integrationist? A real live one? One that believes in mixing *socially* with Negroes, well look at ME. Brother, look at me." Instead of showing anger, most everyone chuckled at this man's impassioned speech.

The congregation voted to back the vestry and not pay the assessment. Their vote, however, was much closer than the vestry's.

The prayers in the service today were almost over. Soon I heard: "The grace of our Lord Jesus Christ, the love of God, and the fellowship of the Holy Ghost, be with us all evermore." When you reach this point in our service, you know it's almost time for the sermon. What will old so-and-so talk about today? For years and years, Charleston people have listened to and joked about the sermons they've heard in this church. Two generations or so ago, they had a preacher who either could not remember the names of the people he quoted or he would make up the quotations himself; for he always began his quotations with, "As another has said." He came to be known as Brother Another.

But the sermon I heard today was a good one. The new

minister certainly has a talent, I was thinking to myself. He was accusing us of being a "Christian" aristocracy, but he managed to do so in such a way that we laughed at ourselves. In the course of his sermon, he defined love as "activated concern." St. Thomas' already contributes financially to St. Paul's. Now maybe someday I'll be able to introduce this congregation to the mission center *people* and really give them a chance to activate their concern and show their Christian love. God, I'm a dreamer. But the world takes all kinds, right? Right.

I guess I had overestimated my importance among the people at church today. Before I went, I was sure that I would be confronted with racial arguments. Instead, after church was over, no one seemed particularly interested in talking with me about anything, though everyone was polite. I did talk to one gentleman for a while. In the course of the conversation he asked me how everything was at the bank, unaware that I had left it two years ago.

"By the way, William," my father said at dinner, "you had better see about buying a graveyard plot soon if you want to be buried at St. Thomas'. They're running out of space."

Since I do want to be buried there, I called the man in charge this afternoon.

It's Sunday night. We've been in Charleston a little more than a week. One of my anxieties has been relieved. The center does not seem to have any connection with the organized civil rights movement. Instead of Father Andrews's expecting me to become involved in that movement, he has practically ignored me altogether. I get the idea that he's watching me to see what I will do on my own. Though I still do not know how I will spend my time this summer, I must say that I like the freedom Father Andrews' approach gives me.

I'm beginning to worry about something else, however. There seems to be a danger of the center's being too paternalistic. It is financed by wealthy white people many of whom are strong segregationists. The children are taught and guided by educated whites and Negroes who come from outside the ghetto. Money, clothes, and food are given to the needy to help them over temporary situations. As far as I can tell, there is very little indigenous leadership from the people of the neighborhood. The parents of the kids seem either to work all day or to sit in their doorways, watching the traffic go by. The *issue* of segregation appears to be far removed from their minds. That's not to say that these people don't feel suppressed. Everyone, from the children in the chapel to the four angry men in the automobile, feels the suppression that the segregated system brings upon them. But there is no open talk of fighting for one's rights. Not once have I heard the mention of the name of any civil rights leader, not even Dr. King's. The people of this neighborhood seem to accept their servile position. Their frustrations and hostility remain dangerously subconscious. And this is, at least partially, the result of "dead-end" paternalism.

A valuable service is provided by paternalism. I'm not about to discount it altogether. When a child is hungry and someone gives him food to eat, that's good. When a parent is too busy or too irresponsible to raise a son and the Head Start program attempts to do the job, that's good. When the electricity is cut off in someone's home on account of non-payment and Father Andrews pays the bill, that's good. But if paternalism is made an end in itself as it has been in Charleston, the child will continue to stand a good chance of going hungry, of not receiving guidance from his own parents. The electricity will continue to be cut off. True paternalism, or fatherliness, is, however, not an end in itself. The good father raises his children so that when they come of age they will leave him and cleave to their husbands and wives. And it is the sons and daughters who must decide, finally, when they have come of age. Not the father!

In our present-day society, white people like me who are haunted by the race problem and who would like to do something personally seem to have only two choices: one, they can identify themselves completely with the civil rights movement; two, they can continue to dole out hand-me-down clothes, food, and money in the traditional paternalistic fashion. I cannot see myself identifying completely with the organized civil rights movement — there's too much of the old white South in me for that — and I suspect that the movement would not touch me if I were only half committed to it. At the same time, I can already see the destructiveness of dead-end paternalism. Thus, I am driven to a third choice. Cannot we who are concerned become *personally* involved with Negroes without marching in the streets? Couldn't we tutor children having trouble in school? Couldn't we teach older boys how to drive? Couldn't we take kids out in the country on picnics? Couldn't we, in time, provide training schools for those who would be able to work in the new industry coming to town? Couldn't we, like Linda and Sally, work professionally with Negroes? The list of fatherly things we could do is endless. Each day we'd be required to say: "My work is a means to an end. I am looking forward to the day when the people of this ghetto can help themselves. When that time comes, I will expect them to walk away from me, just as the daughter leaves her father in our wedding service."

The ghetto kids desperately need fatherliness! The adults need help too. St. Paul's Mission is one of the few places in town making any effort to meet those needs, and it is faced with the danger of corrupting fatherliness into dead-end paternalism. The question in my mind right now is this: Can white Charleston help meet the needs of black Charleston in a way that is permanently helpful to the Negro? Can those people at St. Thomas' and those people on the yacht activate their concern and help the Negro help himself?

Or is too late? Has the segregated, paternalistic system driven the Negro too far away from the white man? Has white Charleston become, as Brian seems to think it has, so smug in its ways that it can no longer hear the cry exhaled by the people of the ghetto, the children of the mission center? Is Cousin Lois wrong? Is it too late to do the right thing?

III

Laughing and Weeping

There was a nice sand beach ahead of us and clear water in front of that. Officer and petty officer wives were stretched out on the sand, enjoying the South Carolina sun. Suddenly, our kids had on their bathing suits and were running, full speed, for the water. Was this another Northern invasion? Was it a swim-in? What was this horde of running, shouting children? Bewildered, the white bathers divided, like the Red Sea waters, as fifty black bodies, with Linda and me in the middle, crossed the beach and hit the water, screaming! I stopped for a quick moment when I came to the edge of the lake. Fifty wild colored children in the water, disapproving whites on the shore. I swallowed hard before I jumped in; but I did jump in. I had to. There were only three of us who swam, Linda, myself, and one of the boys. I had to.

For everything there is a season, and a time
      for every matter under heaven:
a time to be born, and a time to die;
a time to plant, and a time to pluck up what
      is planted;
a time to kill, and a time to heal;
a time to break down, and a time to build up;
a time to weep, and a time to laugh;
a time to mourn, and a time to dance;
a time to cast away stones, and a time to
      gather stones together;
a time to embrace, and a time to refrain
      from embracing;
a time to seek, and a time to lose;
a time to keep, and a time to cast away;
a time to rend, and a time to sew;
a time to keep silence, and a time to speak;
a time to love, and a time to hate;
a time for war, and a time for peace.
What gain has the worker from his toil?

— *Ecclesiastes*

JUNE 20: The theme for the worship service and the class this morning was the Eighth Commandment, "Thou shalt not steal." Before coming to work at the center this summer, I thought that stealing would be a major problem among the people of the ghetto. For the first two or three days, I locked up my car; but since that time, I haven't bothered to. The children like to play inside it — the boys pretending that it's an airplane, the girls, a dollhouse — but no one has taken anything yet, not even my flashlight or first-aid kit. Linda often leaves money on her desk during her lunch hour. She says that occasionally someone will take a quarter or a dollar, but most of the time, no one touches the money. Nevertheless, I thought it would be profitable to spend the morning on stealing.

A firm believer in visual aids for sermonettes, I got a Ping-Pong ball, a shiny stapler, a flashlight, a basketball, a coat, and a set of car keys and placed them all around the chapel, on the back row, on the altar, on the prayer desk. In order to show how stealing little things leads to stealing bigger things, I pretended to be a shoplifter; and when no one was looking, I swiped the items one by one and concealed them under my roomy cassock. With each theft, the congregation clapped their hands. By the time I got to the car keys, my cassock now bulging with the basketball, the applause was thunderous. I was having so much fun that it did not occur to me that my sermonette might be doing more harm than good.

But in the class that followed, I really began to worry about the value of such a teaching device. As soon as we got into the classroom, the kids could not wait to tell me the various things which they'd stolen. They teach us at seminary to try to get people to be open with you; they do not tell us what you do next. The class said that they'd stolen at various times plums, sodas, footballs, firecrackers, dresses, canned foods. They particularly enjoyed recounting the thefts from white merchants. When I asked them what happens when they get caught, one said, "The white man takes us aside and shakes his finger at us and tells us he's going to call the police next time, but he never does." Another said that he'd been taken to the police station and then let go. When I asked them if they thought it was right to steal, they giggled. One girl said, "If you steal from a white man, it's all right." "It ain' all right ever to steal from nobody," Sneed interrupted. "What's so bad about being a white man?" I asked, pretending to be serious. They giggled some more.

The class, which is up to eighteen, started getting out of hand, so I read them a story from some church educational series about a little white girl with pigtails who couldn't make up her mind who to have to her birthday party and her mother had limited her to fifteen people and what should she do. My class quieted down.

I guess I must have been both right and wrong about stealing. While stealing does appear to be a problem, it seems to be more of a game than a criminal act. Some people have birthday parties; some people shoplift things when the white merchant isn't looking.

This afternoon I had great plans for organizing the Boy Scout troop. Sixteen had signed up for it; but when the appointed hour came, only six came to the meeting, three of whom I recruited at the last minute from the horseshoe pit. I'm afraid these fellows spotted my lack of enthusiasm, which tends to vary according to numerical success. After a brief meeting, I made no more attempt during the rest of the day to do anything constructive. The hours passed slowly. The heat, the boredom won possession of me. I withdrew into myself and did not even pay attention to the games of Ping-Pong that I played, and invariably lost.

June 21. My class today was helped out by Gloria, a girl of unusual maturity and leadership for a fourteen-year-old. It began like this:

TEACHER. Today, we will talk about the Ninth Commandment.
GLORIA. When you get through with that, there's something I want to ask you about.
TEACHER. Ask it now.
GLORIA. Well, okay. Yesterday, a fifteen-year-old boy on a bicycle stopped Charlene and me and asked us why we went to Bible School. He said that it was for little children and laughed at us. What would you have said to him?

TEACHER. (*Great, I thought to myself, this is what I've been waiting on, a role play.*) Tell you what, Gloria, I'll pretend like I'm this boy riding on my bicycle, stopping and asking you the same question. Let's see what you can do with it. Here goes.

BOY. Hey, girl, what you doin' goin' to Bible School. Das for little children.

GLORIA. O, year! The Bible's for everybody. I go there to learn about God.

BOY. Man, what you want to learn about God for. He ain' never done nuttin' for you.

GLORIA. Boy, where you think that bicycle comes from?

BOY. He come from me Ma. (*They laughed at my use of that word.*)

GLORIA. Where you think your Ma got it from?

BOY. She get 'em from work, hard work, that's where.

GLORIA. Who'd the person get the money from to pay your Ma?

BOY. I guess he got 'em from de person dat paid him.

GLORIA (*pointing her finger at me*). Now, tell me, boy, where'd that person get the money from?

TEACHER (*running out of arguments against this young theo-logian-lawyer, who was proving to me God's causality of every-thing*). That's good, Gloria, now who else wants to try?

I let Sneed and several other boys play the role of Gloria, and I continued to be the bad guy. The next step is to let them play both roles. After that was over, we somehow got on the passage from the Bible (I've forgotten which book it's in) on there's a time for livin' and a time for dyin', a time for gladness and a time for sadness. As Gloria started repeating

in paraphrase form this passage, she began to give the words a
little rhythm, then more, then a lot of rhythm:

> There's a time to eat and a time to drink
> A time to do and a time to think.
> (The class began to clap and join in.)
> There's a time for reapin' and a time to sow
> A time for rakin' and a time to mow.
> (I was standing up leading the clapping.)
> There's a time for walkin' and a time for flyin'
> There's a time for livin' and a time for dyin'.
> A time for laffin' and a time for weepin'
> A time for prayin' and a (clap, clap) time for sweepin'.
> (We were running out of rhymes.)
> A time to jump and a time for prancin'
> A time for walkin' and a (clap, clap) time for dancin'.

Two or three of the boys took this last piece of Biblical wisdom quite seriously and started dancing around, doing the
jerk. The singing had turned into loud shouting. So I had to
put an end to it. I remember reading somewhere that the liturgy should be the spontaneous expression of the people as
they worship God. I didn't agree with that statement at the
time, sounded too wild, but here I was, doing my best to put it
into practice. We finished the class with a few verses of
"Every Time I Feel the Spirit."

And this afternoon I got the spirit, so much so that I
cleaned out the recreation equipment and junk closet, which
looked as if it hadn't been touched since some well-meaning
white person gave the mission its first broken record-player.
Father Andrews, Linda, and Sally all complimented me on
the work I did. Seems like I'm an expert at throwing out junk.
I told myself as I threw away the broken stuff that if we're to

produce organized youth, we must organize their surroundings. That's good, I thought. Thursday, I'll plan for the Bible School to clean up the whole mission. Adam, the caretaker-janitor, thought that was another "fine idea."

There's a corner grocery store in my parents' section of town, run by two Greeks, which, I discovered tonight, they've been running for fifty years. I knew that store had been there for a long time, ever since I could remember. Most of the kids from my section of town spend their early years at East Bay Playground and on the way home stop at Spiro's for a Pepsi-Cola. Now it is quite an art to get a Pepsi from Spiro or his brother without paying for it. In fact, the only time I ever tried, I got caught and wasn't able to return for a week. Throughout the years, the boys have cheated Spiro, and Spiro has gotten even by raising the prices that the boys' parents pay for odds and ends they need to buy after all the other stores in town are closed.

A stranger could probably guess the great age of this store merely by seeing the layers of rust on the tops of many of the cans. I remember one time being quite hostile while several such strangers, Yankee tourists, were in Spiro's making fun not only of the rusty cans but also of the window decorations that hadn't been changed in years, and the dust and the cobwebs. Why I was hostile, I don't know; Spiro hasn't said twenty words to me in the years that I've been going in his store, except to quote prices and count out the change. But I remember thinking that by God, if those Yankees don't like Spiro's, they could go elsewhere, hopefully home, and take their loud, obnoxious talk with them.

Tonight Spiro's was a changed place. The cans hadn't been replaced, and I wouldn't swear that the floor had been swept, but right there in the middle of the main counter between the Real Kill and the potato chips was a large silver tray, a worn red ribbon tied to it, on which was written: "Happy Fiftieth Anniversary from Your Boys." When I asked Spiro about it, he beamed as he told me how the people of Charleston, young boys and their fathers, had several weeks ago given his brother and himself a party and presented them with this tray. Then he told me how in preparation they had decorated the window with artificial fruit and how the mayor of Charleston, being one of the boys, had been there too. When Spiro was adding up the groceries on the bag that he would put them in, it occurred to me that he was old, very old indeed.

I told my wife about the anniversary party when I got home and how I didn't know why I was so moved by it. "William," she said, "that could only happen in a place like Charleston." Seems like lots of things can only happen in Charleston.

June 22. I'm finding that the worship services provide an excellent opportunity to experiment with the liturgy. There are no fussy people around to complain to the bishop about the young minister who changes the rubrics or asks the congregation questions in the middle of the service, or just does things they aren't accustomed to. Today, I had three of the kids act out a short play to illustrate what bearing false witness against one's neighbor is. It went very well and would have been better if it hadn't been for Richard, the retarded boy who chases street sweepers, who today for the first time blessed us with his presence for the worship and who interrupted every once in a while with a religious sound or some other expressive word. The play went something like this:

PREACHER. Our young actors will now act out the Ninth Commandment.
ALFRED. I don't like that girl there (*pointing to Terry*). Let's see, what can I do to hurt her. I know. I'll pretend like she stole ten cents out of my mother's pocketbook.
(*Enter Mother, nine years old.*)
ALFRED. Mother, Mother, Terry stole ten cents out your pocketbook.
TERRY. I did not.
ALFRED. Yes, you did.
RICHARD. Let us pray.
TERRY (*very emphatically*). I most certainly did not.
ALFRED. Yes, you did. I seen you reach in dere and take 'um, just as sho' as my name is Alfred Brown. (*He was ad-libbing.*)
MOTHER. You bad, bad chile.
RICHARD. Amen.
MOTHER. You steal money from me, I'm goin' to give you a good whuppin'. Come here to me.
TERRY (*walking away in fear and trembling, holding back a big laugh*). But, but, but . . .

I took over at that point and tried to connect the play with Judas's betrayal of Jesus. Richard settled down pretty well on the chancel rail and let me preach. However, when we started practicing the Commandments with the congregation repeating them after me, he joined in again. By the time we got to adultery, the congregation was once again laughing dangerously loud. I stopped the recitation and putting my hand on Richard's shoulder said, "You laugh at Richard, but he's worshiping in his way, just as you are worshiping in your way." I was quite pleased with this thoughtful statement of mine about po' little Richard and beamed self-righteously as I spoke. But I overlooked one thing. Richard somehow understood what I was talking about and started worshiping even louder — and in his own way. It went like this:

PREACHER. Thou shalt not bear false witness.
RICHARD. OUR FATHER.
CONGREGATION. Thou shalt not bear false witness.
RICHARD. LET US PRAY.
PREACHER. Thou shalt not covet.
RICHARD. FUCK.
CONGREGATION. Thou shalt not covet. Ho! Ho! Ho!
And so forth.

After the service, Richard forced his way into the class and, for some unknown reason, was very quiet. Even during the handicraft period — the worst mess yet, paint, crayons, clay, *ack*, terrible — Richard said not a word. When we went down to the corner lot to play baseball, Richard followed us and caught for one team. He did such a good job that the boys let him bat. Surprisingly enough, he got a hit. It took three of his teammates to steer and push him to first base, but he did make it, and later he scored a run.

This afternoon, I thought I'd brag on Richard and said in front of him to Linda and Sally, "You should have seen Richard get a hit today. Man, was he one proud Dodger." No response from Richard. "He really did well." Still no response. "How 'bout that, Richard, how'd it feel?" (And then, slapping him on the back), "Come on, Richard, tell us about it." But little retarded Richard, with his moth-eaten shirt and his decaying teeth, was miles away.

June 23. So far this week, the recreation inventory is down one basketball, the same one I "stole" in chapel, six darts, four Ping-Pong balls, one large glass of marbles — not bad when you consider how much these items are used and how many different people use them.

Our clean-up today was a success. About seventy percent of the Bible School showed up and worked and played for two hours. I worked harder than anyone. Father Andrews was watching me from a distance. I wonder what he thought about my taking the clean-up so enthusiastically. Was I trying to prove to the kids and to him that I am not above doing dirty work? Or, was I trying to prove this to me? Adam got energetic himself and for the first time in weeks, maybe months, mopped and waxed the floor. I drove him to a Negro public school, where he has a friend who sneaked us out the wax.

Sally, now in charge of Head Start, and I had a bag lunch together outside in the shade on the Big Flat, an ancient tombstone so named because of its shape. Richard had some of our bag lunch with us. Since we're planning a big Bible School picnic for tomorrow, Sally and I tried to tell Richard to be sure to come. The word "picnic" seemed to mean nothing to Richard; the word "swimming" did. "Swummin', swummin'," he muttered all through lunch. Sally seems discouraged by the disorganization of the Head Start program;

but as I told her, when you compare her kids to mine, she looks as though she's running a precision drill team. The person entombed under our table died in the 1850's and was probably no great success because the epitaph on his tomb read, "He did the best he could." Sally hasn't figured Father Andrews out either but tells me not to underestimate him. "He's one of the smartest people I know, white or colored."

After lunch, the day dragged. I found myself falling into the do-nothing mood again. I even went down to the corner where the biggest bums, most of whom Father Andrews has kicked out of the center, hang out. The conversations on this corner are as dull and limited as many conversations in my night world. Instead of "Your great-great-uncle never said a curse word," I was listening to, "Cheby got hole of some sherry last night and he's still in bed this afternoon." My feet dangled over the side of the wall, and I watched with little interest the life of the Negro ghetto go by: little children chasing each other, middle-aged women laughing together as they strolled lazily by, the same women I hear from my bedroom window early in the morning when they are walking to work, a very old man without teeth, pushing a heavy cart of discarded clothes up the inclined street — the great sun scorching everyone and burning up whatever ambition and enthusiasm there might be.

It was a long time until six when we close the center.

June 24. What a day this has been! Last night, right before closing, I brought half a bushel of peaches into the center for the Bible School picnic that we had today. Robert, a sixteen-year-old whom I've been trying to teach how to drive, was playing pool. He saw me coming, met me at the door, and without a word started helping himself to the peaches.

"Stop that!" I said. "What do you think you're doing?"

Robert grinned.

"I'm serious. Put those peaches back."

Robert did not grin that time.

"I try to teach you how to drive, I try to work for you and, by God, I expect some co-operation and some interest in the center out of you." — I pointed my finger at him — "Pal, in this world, you've got to work as well as take."

Robert looked down at the floor, then glanced toward me and said, "Man, you jammin' me," then walked out of the center. I didn't ask him what "jammin'" meant. I was too mad to care.

This morning when I arrived at the center, I found out what Robert had meant. The place had been broken into during the night. The items that were stolen were enough to convince me who had done it. The symbol of our argument, the basket of peaches, was gone. The hot dogs, the loss of which would, in Robert's eyes, halt the picnic were also stolen. Lastly, one bag of potato chips, which taste good after a few beers at night, was gone. Nothing else. The recreation equipment closet that I had cleaned up was torn up, but that was all. "Jammin'" is putting someone else in such a position that he feels as though he must express hostility toward you, yet he can't. He must, but he can't. He is jammed into a corner and can't get out. He must, but he can't. Robert finally did release his hostility by breaking into the center and striking at me, and thus he did get out of the corner. When I get mad, I try to jam people, leaving them helpless; when

Robert gets mad, he steals and destroys. We aren't so different.

I didn't let this incident get me too upset, however; for today was the long-awaited day of the big picnic. I hurried to the store, replaced the stolen items, and watched the children arrive. Most of them, usually late for Bible School, were half an hour early. Sneed, Gloria, Edward, who is the one the others call "Black-y-mo," in fact, all the kids that I'm getting to know well were there, all except Richard. Even though they were terribly excited — it was the first time in a year that the center has sponsored such a picnic — they muffled their enthusiasm when we told them they would have to be very orderly if they wanted to go on the picnic. Somehow, I felt as though we were playing cat-and-mouse with these kids, making them be so unnaturally quiet and holding the picnic over their heads like a guillotine. Hell, why shouldn't they make some noise? Didn't they know that we were only bluffing? That we weren't about to leave anyone behind?

Father Andrews arrived at ten o'clock and said that he'd have the transportation for us in a few minutes. When I told him about the break-in, I guess I sounded overanxious because he laughed loudly. "William," he said, "you're just beginning to get baptized into the life of this neighborhood. Ho! Ho! Ho!" I didn't tell him who I thought had done it. "See that little boy there with the big smile —" he was pointing across the room as he spoke — "he may well have been the one who broke in. Any one of them could have done it. That's the way life is around here."

An hour later, the first car appeared. It was a station wagon that belongs to the Roman Catholic nun who runs another mission center nearby. A little later, a second station wagon, owned by the ex-president of the South Carolina NAACP arrived. Finally, a shiny new Oldsmobile with Mrs. Andrews at the wheel rolled up. "Are you ready to go?" Father Andrews asked me. "You mean get all these children in three cars, you're joking." I was stunned. But he wasn't joking, and we did get all of them in. Linda, who took the little children, had twenty-four in the station wagon that she drove. I took fourteen boys in the one I had, and Mrs. Andrews took eight or nine girls in the Olds. Besides the boys, I also took the food and ice that Mrs. Martin had carefully packed for us.

Our destination was thirty miles away. We couldn't get the windows open in the back of the station wagon, we got lost in heavy traffic twice, it must have been ninety-five degrees, and one boy had to go to the bathroom so badly that he went on the side of the road when I stopped to ask directions. In spite of all that unpleasantness, there was hardly a sound during the first part of the trip. But, as we began to approach our destination, a military recreation area on a lake, the kids showed some excitement, made some noise, then more, then more and more. I found myself becoming equally excited.

By the time I stopped the car in the parking lot, we were all screaming with joy. There was a nice sand beach ahead of us and clear water in front of that. Officer and petty officer wives were stretched out on the sand, enjoying the South Carolina sun. Suddenly, our kids had on their bathing suits and were running, full speed, for the water. Was this another Northern invasion? Was it a swim-in? What was this horde of running, shouting children? Bewildered, the white bathers divided, like the Red Sea waters, as fifty black bodies, with Linda and me in the middle, crossed the beach and hit the water, screaming! I stopped for a quick moment when I came to the edge of the lake. Fifty wild colored children in the water, disapproving whites on the shore. I swallowed hard before I jumped in; but I did jump in. I had to. There were only three of us who swam, Linda, myself, and one of the boys. I had to.

It's always that first step that's the hardest. Once in, I enjoyed the water as much as the kids. They were jumping off my shoulders, splashing me, ducking me; I was showing off my water tricks for them. Together, we were cooled; together, washed; together, made one — and all by the same water. Finally, when we came out, we cooked the hot dogs and ran around like crazy. Except for the fact that the charcoal was wet and the hot dogs didn't get cooked very much, the day was a great success. Chomping down on one of the black and raw hot dogs, Sneed remarked that we were "having a *real* picnic."

As I limped into the center after it was all over, sunburned and exhausted, Father Andrews laughed at me once again, this time warmly, and told me I looked terrible. I guess I did, but I felt good. "Father Andrews," I said, "if you think I was baptized this morning when I found out about the break-in, you should have seen me and the water rites at the lake today." He laughed again and seemed delighted that we had had such a good time. He told me that we could take as many trips as I wished, though places were hard to find, and we'd been asked by special invitation to go this one time to the military recreation area.

On the way home, I thought to myself that I had taken today what Kierkegaard called a "leap of faith" when I jumped into that water. There was no turning back. And then, almost in the same moment, I remembered that I had to go to two cocktail parties over the weekend and listen to descriptions of swimming pools in peoples' backyards, to accounts of deep sea fishing trips, and to conversations about how little various young wives are paying their maids and how the husbands of these wives think that fellow in the White House is an "s.o.b." And I knew that I'd probably smile and be as polite as anyone there.

June 25. No entry.

June 26. It's Sunday afternoon. Everyone in my parents' house is sleeping except me. Since it took until nine-thirty Friday night to write the above entry, we were able to go to the first cocktail party only for a short time. It was given by some Navy people for their Charleston and Navy friends — "to get them together." The Navy people talked to each other about officer clubs and submarines. The Charleston people talked to themselves about such matters as I had predicted. I sort of floated back and forth between the two groups like an ice cube in a shaky Old-Fashioned glass, slowly tearing up the napkins around my drinks, smiling, looking stupid.

But the cocktail party last night was quite different. We had such a good time that I didn't get up early enough for church this morning. To begin with, it was given by old Charleston people, some of the few who managed to hold on to their money during the Civil War and Reconstruction days, people who fight to avoid any label of ostentation, people who preserve the best of the aristocracy — each taking pride in his particular position, from the lord and lady of the manor to the butler and the maids, each showing great respect for the others — people unthreatened, who have no reason to be defensive about Charleston and who consequently can talk rationally to most everyone to the extent of making even a fellow like me feel at home.

And then too at this party was the crowd of boys I grew up with and their wives. It was the first time this summer that I had seen all of them together. I talked to the wives first. Instead of having to listen to talk about maids twice our age, I found myself doing most of the talking, trying to sell my solution to the race problem, which I now call "transitional paternalism," pleading that we have a duty to try to provide something like a parental influence for the neglected Negro children, until the time they can stand on their own feet and walk away. The three wives I talked with said that they agreed with me completely. One said that she had changed a lot on the racial question in the last few years. She told me how when she first met Father Andrews at a church meeting, she would not shake hands with him, not that she didn't like him, but to shake hands with a Negro. . . . She couldn't do it. But she told me that things were different now. I had almost forgotten the importance of the symbol of shaking hands between the races. That's one I've never been troubled with. The wives were encouraging. None volunteered to help. And I didn't ask.

Two or three drinks later, I sat down and talked to one of the husbands, my old friend Clayton, now doing a residency here at the medical school hospital. Clayton has been conducting a one-man boycott against the movie theaters because of their policy of allowing Negroes to sit downstairs with the white customers. This has been going on for four or five years. He broke his rule once to see a particularly good movie but only after checking at the ticket window to make sure no Negroes were sitting downstairs — they weren't. "Clayton," I said, "I understand that you're becoming more and more conservative while I'm becoming more and more liberal. Before you know it, we're going to meet at the other side of the circle."

"Yes." He laughed as he spoke. "I had to join the White Citizen's Council to save the country from Communists like you."

"Are you serious?" I wasn't sure.

"Yes, I joined it for a while when I was in Greenville, but those fellows are too much even for me. They think Washington is being run by Moscow. I'm probably just as conservative as they are, but I don't believe all that crap. Washington is wrong and full of dishonest politicians, opportunists; that's all."

Clayton, a tall, pleasant-looking man, one of the nicest there, then told me a long story that had come from an ex-FBI agent about how the FBI's files are loaded with records of Martin Luther King's subversive activities. He said that Hoover had brought this information to the attention of the President, who in turn consulted Roy Wilkins, who said that if the President allowed this sort of thing to come out in the open, it would destroy the whole civil rights movement. "That," Clayton said, "would ruin the President's legislation program and ruin him politically; that makes me sick."

I suggested that even if this story were true, King's possible involvement with the Communists should not be so surprising. "Clayton," I said, "we have a potentially revolutionary situation on our hands." Then I told him about the kids who didn't know how to play baseball, who didn't know how to swim, how there was nothing for the older ones and, in many cases, their fathers, to do. And concluding, I said, "I wouldn't find it at all surprising if the civil rights movement and the Communists have some sort of an alliance. Hell, if I was doomed to spend my life on a doorstep, I'd probably try Communism, or anything new for that matter. That's the price we'll have to pay for prejudice and apathy. If your FBI man is right, I just hope King is using the Communists more than they are using him." Clayton nodded his head as though in agreement, or maybe he was merely being polite.

We stopped for a minute to have some pickled shrimp and roasted crab claws that Emily, the maid, was passing around. Then Clayton started talking again. He told me how the civil rights movement was an infringement on peoples' individual rights; how, with projects like the anti-poverty program, the government was trying to blend us into a personality-less gray; how each person is being required to suck the tit of Mother Government; how Washington was destroying individual initiative; how Negroes are just not equal to the Caucasian race. "And why doesn't that Negro on the doorstep you're talking about go out and get his own job?" He spoke openly, calmly, and with at least some objectivity. Then he said, "But you know, William, there's one thing I've overlooked. I haven't tried to see the thing through the colored man's eyes."

I was so eager to speak about another point he'd made that at the time I missed the significance of this last statement. If only Clayton, and myself as well, could genuinely see the civil rights movement, see America through the Negro's eyes! So much of the problem is white arrogance, which, by its very nature, prevents us from putting ourselves in the position of our fellow man, prevents us from having sensitivity to his personal needs, from feeling as the Negro man feels when he sits on the back of the bus, when he is treated rudely at a movie ticket window. It is arrogance that prevents us from understanding what happens to the manhood of the Negro when he is called "Boy" by a white man, in front of his own children. Clayton would be a good man to have on my side.

But the conversations in that fine old home were not all about race. Charleston is famous for its "characters," people who would be rejected by other societies because of their eccentricities (like wearing sandals with tuxedos, crashing parties and insulting the hostesses, fist fighting in the fanciest clubs). Not only are they not rejected in Charleston, they are revered. They are the Rhett Butlers of the twentieth century, the Richards of my night world. When we weren't engaged in serious conversation last night, one of these characters kept us entertained with wonderfully told stories of South Carolina politics and parties. Eccentric characters. Maybe that's why they were so nice to me.

God! I have just received the first truly hard blow in my struggle this summer, one that made me hurt badly on the inside. A close friend of mine, a person as kind as Mrs. Martin, as strong as Clayton, has refused, in a conversation over the telephone, to let me take *one* carload of the boys from the center for a day's picnic at his large country place. Something about how the caretaker would not understand. I had counted so much on using his place this summer. I didn't see how we could be refused. Maybe if my friend had seen the fun these boys had on the big picnic, heard the roar of their excitement as they hit the water, maybe if he'd watched them worship, he would not be so concerned with what his caretaker might think. What an evil, dirty thing racial prejudice is. I know how Robert felt now when I was "jammin'" him. I'd like to express my hostility, but I don't know how. What good would it do anyway? And who is really at fault? My friend? The caretaker? The whole damn South? Me, for promising the boys without asking? Mankind? I'd like to tell him to go to hell, tell somebody to go to hell. But who? How? I'd like to get out of the corner, but I can't. Ever since I promised to take them, the boys have been talking about the fishing and swimming they would do. I should have asked sooner. Now what can I do? Where can I take them? Is there nowhere to go? God, help us. If this friend will not have us, who will? God, forgive us for racism. Maybe this transitional paternalism idea of mine, which people agree with intellectually, isn't worth the effort. Genteel aristocracy, fine old homes, eccentric characters, pickled shrimp: CRAP. Maybe the wing of the civil rights movement which regards the conservative white man as an enemy to be defeated is the only answer. Maybe all this acceptance I've been getting around town is a lot of crap. God. . . . Goddammit.

June 27. What a discouraging day! Still upset from yesterday, I didn't have my heart in my work today. Furthermore, now that the Bible School is over, Father Andrews has provided me *no* structure to work in. I might as well have spent the day on the corner with the bums and let the rest of the world go by.

My visit to the diocesan office didn't help matters. I went there to ask if *they* could find some place, any place, for me to take the children on all-day trips. "I want to teach them how to start fires and how to swim, if possible." The diocese was sympathetic but said that they knew of no place. The diocese owns a summer camp on an island thirty or forty miles south of Charleston. "How about there?" I asked.

"No, it's against the rules of the camp for anyone to go there when the camp is in session. Besides, the sight of colored children on the beach would probably ruin the work the church has done to promote better race relations. You're from Charleston, William, you ought to know that this thing is dynamite."

"But I thought the camp was to be integrated this year."

"That's right, it is. And if you take fifty colored children down there for a picnic, it won't be integrated any longer. In fact, there won't be a camp there any longer. William, you have to use your head. You're on the right track, but you can't change the way people are overnight. All but eight of the churches in the diocese voted to open the camp to both races rather than close it down. Now it *is* true that the number of children going to camp this summer has dropped, but the camp *will* be integrated. One is there right now, in fact. But you can't push people too hard."

"Where can I take the kids I work with, the kids I'm responsible for? Answer me that. I'm not particularly interested in integrating the camp right now. I only want those boy and girls to have some fun. Fun!"

"Sure you do. We want them to have fun too. But the problem is much more complicated than you'd like to believe. Even if the local church people went along, the white farmers and workers who live on islands near where the camp is located would be apt to cause serious trouble."

The people at the diocese did agree to discuss the matter further and see if they could locate a place for us to go.

*

June 28. Today started off brighter but ended as dark as yesterday, though for a different reason. And it could have been far worse if it hadn't been for Father Andrews and Mrs. Martin. I started the day with all sorts of ideas of how to get things moving around the center. Instead of spending all of my time working with the boys and girls, I'm going to devote some of it to planning, in the seclusion of the library, well-organized activities for them. Right away, I set up the structure for the first such activity, to which I have given the original name, the Boys Club. It will meet every afternoon for two or three hours with carefully planned things to do. Within the Boys Club, I hope to include Boy Scouts, boxing, if Brian will ever come through, exercises, baseball, maybe even a worship service. I think I will limit it to boys ages ten to fifteen. You have to start somewhere.

At the appointed hour this afternoon, twelve fellows showed up. They elected Sneed president, who, by the way, knows more baseball rules than I do now, and a boy they call "Teet" vice-president. (Teet was given that name because he "ain' got no teet' in he mout'.") They all seemed interested and enthusiastic. But when I took them outside to demonstrate how to pitch a tent, the trouble started. Maybe the tent I brought was too big and too fancy, I don't know. Anyway, a boy who, I found out later, is named Zookie, a boy who is sixteen and hangs out with the shoe repair shop gang around the corner, saw us from the street and joined us. I told him that I would be glad to have him in the Boys Club except that he's a year too old.

"Boys Club," he sneered, "I'll start my own Boys Club. Here, let me help you put up the tent," he added as he proceeded to help pull it down.

"Come on now, fellow, what you got against us?" I guess my voice sounded sort of whiny.

"I ain' got nothing against you, man, I'm trying to help," he said, imitating my voice and pulling out a tent peg. "See, you had that peg in the wrong place."

"What you do that for!" I yelled.

One of our boys went over and stood by Zookie's side. The rest were quiet and still. He pulled out another tent peg. "I told you, man, I'm trying to set this tent up the right way." His voice was neither loud nor whining but firm and controlled.

"Well, sport, you can get the hell out of here." I walked over to him. He raised the tent peg some, not brandishing it like a weapon but not holding it like a tent peg either. I stopped. And stared at him. He at me. Should I, right now, take a stand to demonstrate to the boys that I am not going to put up with this sort of stuff? Or, should I go get Father Andrews? I hesitated too long. Zookie had me where he wanted me, right over the barrel. He laughed, the bastard. I turned slowly and went for Father Andrews.

In a minute, he and Adam were outside and the bully was gone. "Where is he?" I asked our boys. "What's his name, anyway?"

Jerome started to tell me, but Sneed interrupted. "Don't you say nuttin', boy! Don't you say one word." Though Sneed was right to keep the law of the jungle and not let Jerome betray even the one who was trying to break up their club, I could not help but realize that, in a crisis, I am to the boys — even the ones I know best — just another white man. Then Adam took over and soon found out that it was Zookie who was causing the trouble.

Father Andrews left the center and in a few minutes came back holding Zookie by his collar, pushing him into the center, up to the library. I should have done that, I thought. If I was completely over my prejudice, I would have done just that. Or *was* it prejudice that prevented me from laying a hand on a Negro boy? Maybe I was just scared, "chicken," as the boys probably said later. Fifteen or twenty minutes passed. Zookie the lion came down from the library a lamb. Thank the Lord for Father Andrews. What would I have done if he hadn't been there? He may not be the best organizer in the world, but he certainly stood by me today when I needed him the most.

Right now I feel the way the Jews must have felt when they were kicked out of Israel, their land flowing with milk and honey, into exile in Babylonia — longing for their homeland, knowing that they couldn't return, and at the same time, trying to adjust to the new land without success. I'm disgusted with white Charleston, and disgusted with myself for not doing my job at the mission, for acting like a coward, for letting Zookie run over me. And then, subconsciously at least, I hate having to ask a Negro to help me, even if he is my boss. Nor am I ready to accept the advice he gave me after he sent Zookie home, though intellectually I know it is good advice and well meant. "William," he said, "you've got to slow down some. Don't think you can solve all our problems overnight. When you get to know this area better, you'll understand what happened today. And, William, don't ever let them think that you're not the boss. They'll run all over you if they get the chance."

I did appreciate Mrs. Martin's help today. About five in the afternoon, she saw me standing alone, watching a Ping-Pong game, my head hung low, my shoulders bent, and invited me into the kitchen for a piece of pie she had made for the children who get lunch neither from the Head Start program nor at home. Without going into details, I told her that I was having a bad day, explaining how everything seems to go wrong at once. She listened, nodding her head, then said, waving her hands, "Just remember, Mr. Barnwell, the Lord makes the back to bear the burden."

I didn't tell Mrs. Martin, but I've heard my mother say the same thing, and she got it from "Ma," her grandmother. I wonder who said it first, the white or the colored people. Thank you, Mrs. Martin, for that, and thank you, Lord.

June 29. Today was better. Or was it? Father Andrews and Adam were nicer than ever. Linda was kind when I described yesterday to her. She told me how even Father Andrews had had to build up an image of authority in this neighborhood; how, when he first started running the center, the boys would let the air out of his tires; how Adam, who was about Zookie's age then, had been one of his biggest problems.

And the boys didn't seem to have lost *too* much respect for me. All returned to the Boys Club meeting today, even the one who had deserted to Zookie.

Brian called while we were in the middle of the meeting and said he could come up to the center right then and give the boxing a try. "Sure," I said, "glad to have you." He explained to the boys how to hold your fists, how to jab with your left, and how to dance with your feet. He had them shadowboxing, running in place, doing push-ups, jumping ropes. A few of the boys wandered off in the middle of the training session, but others took their place. Most of them were attentive throughout. When it was over, we all went into the chapel for a sweaty Compline service.

"Well, what do you think, Brian?" I asked as we were driving home.

"It's not exactly what I had expected."

"What do you mean?"

"Oh, I don't know. I just don't think I'd enjoy working with those boys too much, that's all."

"You mean you didn't like them?"

"Barnwell, I didn't not like them, but it's too drab there at the center or something. Look, I told you I'd coach boxing and I will, but don't expect me to be crazy about them if I'm not."

"There's no point in your working at the center unless you want to."

"Yes, I suppose you are right. Hate to let you down. Guess you think I'm a lousy friend."

"No. Well, I do in a way. But after all, you're the *only* person I've talked to who has made any effort to help." And I told him about not having a place to go and all that.

We shook hands as he got out of the car.

June 30. Drinking half a bottle of whiskey over the course of a night is for me a catharsis. Occasionally I wake up hung-over, but most of the time, like this morning, I awake refreshed and purged of anxiety. After I wrote the entry for the 29th, a fraternity brother from college days who was passing through town stopped by to pay a short visit. He was full of news and stories of mutual friends, and we ended staying up until two. It was great to talk about something other than race.

I knew it was going to be a good day as soon as I turned

onto the street where the center is located. Usually, when I enter the mission neighborhood, I hold my breath much as I did when I went swimming with the kids. I look at the tough, bearded Negro men on the way to work or on the way home after an all-night drunk, the dirty little children, the clothes and sheets flung carelessly over third-story porch banisters to dry, the open windows with no screens; and I mash my lips together. Often I tremble. Once in, I'm all right, the water's good.

Today, however, I was so refreshed and relaxed that I entered the ghetto switching from night into day just as easily as I had consumed all that good Rebel Yell. "Too much and too little wine," wrote Pascal. "Give him none, he cannot find the truth, give him too much, the same." If we're to find truth in this life, we must take some wine along with it, some fun, some laughs. If there is only the depressing ghetto — "drab" as Brian calls it — only friends who disappoint you, only a feeling of personal failure, personal exile, there is no reason to keep searching for the truth of which Pascal speaks.

Shortly after arriving at the center, I received a phone call from the diocese office. While they still could not find me a place to go on all-day picnics, they said that some Episcopalians had donated enough money so that ten or twelve of the mission center kids could get complete scholarships to the two-week camp sessions. They did suggest, though, that I have the parents pay five or ten dollars so that they would have the satisfaction of participating in their child's camp experience. Camp. Oh, the kids'll love it, I thought to myself.

The boys that Brian had coached yesterday came up to me this morning and asked me, *please* Mr. Barnwell, if they could have boxing, not this afternoon, but right then. "Well, boys, how would you like me to coach you?" No, they wanted Brian. "Now, wait boys, I once boxed in the Golden Gloves myself, yes sir, and I earned the title of Windmill Willie." And I proceeded to show how I threw my punches like the arms of a windmill. "We wanta learn 'bout de leff jab, we ain' care nuttin' atall 'bout de windmill." They laughed but finally agreed to give me a try. And it went pretty well for a five-time loser.

This afternoon the Boys Club divided into two groups and had new elections. Sneed was elected chief of the Wildcats, Doug, chief of the Panthers. They said that they wanted to have a contest this afternoon to see who could clean up the center the best. "Great, tell you what, see if you can think of some all-day trip that you'd like to go on, and I'll take the winning group on it next week." No, they couldn't go to the military recreation area and, no, they couldn't go to my friend's lake. The Panthers decided on the state capitol in Columbia; the Wildcats wanted more than anything to cross the Ashley River and spend the day at Skeeter Beach (a slimy, muddy place), where they could catch crabs while the skeeters caught them. Both groups did a good job cleaning up. Linda and I finally judged that Sneed's group had done the better job. With that, Doug and the Panthers became furious and threatened to leave the center and never return. So I promised to take them on a trip too.

IV

The Foolish and the Wise

When you have been raised on the water in this part of the state, you learn from an early age how to walk on oyster shells as you make your way from the bank to the deeper water. . . . I made it to the deep water from the bank without a scratch. Then came William, an eleven-year-old boy who is no larger than my six-year-old nephew. He charged into the water like he was running to first base. I closed my eyes. Is the boy nuts? Doesn't he know what he'll do to his feet? Hasn't he been raised on the water in the Carolina lowcountry, same as me? . . .

Damn the segregated system that keeps my boys from knowing how to walk on oyster shells and keeps me oblivious to the fact that some of them have never seen an oyster shell bank in their lives.

*For consider your call, brethren; not
many of you were wise according to worldly
standards, not many were powerful, not
many were of noble birth; but God chose what
is foolish in the world to shame the wise;
God chose what is weak in the world to shame
the strong, God chose what is low and despised
in the world, even things that are not, to
bring to nothing things that are, so that no
human might boast in the presence of God.*

— I Corinthians

July 1. This morning I gathered as many Wildcats and Panthers as I could find to tell them about the possibility of going to the white camp. Some of them had gone to the other diocesan camp — the Negro one — last summer and wanted to know why it had been closed down. I said I didn't know, though I have heard that it was closed due to "typical Negro mismanagement." "Unfortunately," I went on, "this year only six boys and six girls will be able to go to camp. It's a lot more expensive than the one some of you went to last summer and that's all we have money for." And then I told them that I wanted each to pay at least $5.00 and to talk it over with their parents and somehow we'd figure out who could go. The boys were all tremendously excited and full of questions — all but Chief Panther Doug that is. His eyes fell to the ground and eventually he walked away. Later in the morning I found out the reason why.

It seems that his mother had set aside $7.50 for him to go to the Negro camp this summer. Starting in May, Doug had asked Father Andrews several times when the camp would begin. Each time, apparently Father Andrews gave twelve-year-old Doug some vague, noncommittal answer. Finally, Doug's mother, convinced that there would be no camp for her son this summer, took him to buy some long-needed clothes with the money. The $7.50 is gone. Now, there will be a camp that Doug can go to, a camp much better equipped than the Negro one, a camp on a white sand beach, a place where you can catch all the crabs you can eat. But since the $7.50 is gone, Doug is certain that he has no chance of going to camp. It's too late. It's always too late for a kid like Doug. His life must be one disappointment after another. The seven dollars and fifty goddam cents is gone.

Well, by God, I'll tell you one thing. Doug is going to camp this year if I have to pay the money myself. My friend Clayton, the doctor who's been boycotting movies, admitted that he hadn't tried to see life through the Negro's eyes. If only he could have seen it through Doug's eyes today! I saw through them this morning, perhaps only for a moment, but long enough to realize that getting him to camp is one of the things that really matters in this life, the kind of thing that will give me the strength and courage to stand up and face the unyielding segregationist.

Speaking of segregationists, we received some of their good-will this afternoon, in the form of hand-me-down clothes. These gifts arrive at the center by the barrelful. Half of it is junk and is sent directly to the trash pile and unceremoniously burned; the rest is stored, sometimes for years. The adult Negroes are too proud to take the clothes; the children rarely find anything they want. It is collected mostly by church groups of different denominations, such as the ladies' organization that called today, by people who feel that they are fulfilling their Christian duty by filling our trash pile and our storeroom with garments of another age.

Adam and I drove down to the church on my night side of

town to collect the clothes. We laughed when we saw what was written on the barrel in which the hand-me-downs were placed.

Always
Bring
Clothes to the needy

A. B. C. The racial problem is as simple as that. What could be easier? Dole out old things or old money. You need not get involved with people. The church group today wouldn't even come to the center to bring their junk. At least most will do that. I don't know why I volunteered to go downtown to pick it up. "Adam," I said, "how's it feel to be needy?" He laughed again.

Now I know my abc's. There's a strange similarity between this white church giving and certain government spending on the poor. "Let's vote so many billions of dollars for foreign aid and various domestic poverty programs," decide the liberal Democrats and Republicans. We need not become involved personally. Only be sure you pull the right lever.

I long to be able to preach: *Don't just load the poor down with old clothes and old money. That way they'll always be dependent on you, but do come in person, teach them, teach care of clothing and money. If the most capable of you will do volunteer work and staff such programs as Head Start, we may get somewhere. Your money is not enough.*

But I wasn't as mad today as I sound. In all honesty, I had fun. Adam and I outfitted the little girls in black cocktail dresses that dragged along behind them, high-heeled shoes, funny veiled Easter hats, and we did the boys up in tuxedos, shirts without collars, and glasses with lenses missing. You'd have thought it was Halloween.

My wife has just read the above entry. She tells me that it is as cruel and as arrogant as some of the people I'm fighting against this summer. "You think you know so much and are doing such a great job with all your *personal involvement*. I'll bet those people who collected the clothes went to a lot of trouble. You know, they didn't have to do that. All you want to do is laugh at them. William, I don't understand you sometimes."

July 2. Another one of the activities that I've set up is a sewing class for girls ages ten to eighteen which I've scheduled to meet every Saturday at ten o'clock. We held the organizational meeting last Wednesday. Twelve girls signed their names at the appropriate place on the bulletin board which designated that they would come on Wednesday. Only six attended the meeting. Of those, four had forgotten about the class and had to be brought to the center in my car. But at the end of the meeting, those six were talking about basting and tacking and darting and all sorts of things, and they were eager to come to the class which was to be held today. Cousin Lois and I together found someone to teach the class, a lady named Florence, another distant cousin, who, by the way, is the only person who has volunteered to do work at St. Paul's. I told Florence that I would come to the center about ten today, though we don't normally work on Saturdays, to make sure that everything was going smoothly.

At ten o'clock I was at the center, but the center was closed. What had happened to Adam? He told me that he always kept the center open from nine until two on Saturdays. And what had happened to Florence? I was sure that she would be there on time. And what had happened to the girls? Not one was there. I had pampered these girls last Wednesday just to get them to come, but I figured they would take some initiative and come on their own today. I was wrong. To make matters worse, I couldn't even get inside to cool off in Father Andrews's air-conditioned office. The time passed. It got to be ten-thirty. Still no one. Edward, the boy the fellows call Black-y-mo, showed up and swung back and forth on the gate. I went over to talk with him for a few minutes but couldn't make out what he was saying; he has a terrible speech impediment. The phone began ringing inside. It rang and it rang; but of course I couldn't answer it. Damn it. These girls aren't interested. What do you have to do to get them to help themselves? What do you have to do to get them to come on time when they promised they would? Maybe I don't have enough patience for this work. Maybe I'm not even capable of slowing down as Father Andrews suggested.

Ten forty-five. Still no one. The blasted phone continued to ring. There've been at least three break-ins at the center since I've been working here, and I thought, perhaps I could break in myself and answer that phone. It must be very easy. Seems as if *one* girl would have shown, Gloria, my liturgist, if no one else. How do they expect to be considered equal when they are so irresponsible? My prejudice was making its way to the surface. But then Florence didn't seem too punctual herself, though I was positive it was Florence on the phone. She could have called me earlier if she was not going to be able to come today. Since I didn't have any money on me, I couldn't call her from the New Deal Lunch down the street. And

Adam, is he as irresponsible as the rest? Edward was making mud pies now; it was getting hotter. To hell with it, I'm going home. And I did.

As soon as I could, I got on the phone to try and figure out what had happened. Florence had meant to call sooner to tell me that she had some sick relatives she'd be busy with today; but she didn't. Adam had been given the day off by Father Andrews and both had meant to tell me; but they didn't. As for the girls in the class, God alone knows what happened to them. Perhaps it's a good thing Florence is the one teaching the sewing. As a person who waits until the last minute to cancel a definite engagement, she probably has just the right temperament to work with these Negroes.

July 3. For some reason, every now and then church on Sunday will give me new strength, make me remember how truly fortunate I am, how fine life is. Today, my father and I went to Holy Communion together, and ever since I've been thinking to myself how very close I am to my parents this summer. Instead of causing a rift in the family, my work has brought us together. Up until now, whenever we'd discuss race — and that was often — I would become terribly defensive. Having no outlet for my concern about the Negro situation, concern that is intermixed with guilt, I would try to release my feelings through hot and heavy arguments. Being able to do nothing positive about the situation, I would spend my time verbally running down the South, "decadent, disintegrating, deteriorating" — all the easy clichés — trying without success to relieve my anguish by shifting my guilt to my Charleston friends and family. Such arguments and indictments are introspective and do little, if any, good. Now I've got my sleeves rolled up and am doing something, making many mistakes, loving, hating, doing perhaps only a little, but something worth more than all my tirades about the backward South. There is a certain freedom in me now. I don't feel the same need to tear down. It is a freedom to love.

Reconciliation, like divorce, is always two-sided. My parents are not nearly so defensive with me this summer. When I describe individual situations to them, I find that they respond with sensitivity and concern. Now if I told them I was taking a bunch of kids to the white camp to help integrate it in order to help achieve social justice, they'd become emotional and cut me off. But if I tell them about how much camp means to twelve-year-old Doug, a boy who thinks of $7.50 as a thousand dollars, I find that they forget about race and social issues and see before them a young fellow with a face, a thin brown face with a hurt expression, a young fellow with a body, a personality all of his own, a person like them — or me. Instead of talking about the big things, we talk about how we can get Doug adequately clothed for camp. My parents can cry, exactly like me, while society crucifies its little children. And they do cry. How can they activate their concern? And do more than hand down old clothes? In our Communion service, we are made one with each other, one with Christ; and then we ask God to assist us with his grace that we may continue in that holy fellowship and do all such good works as he has prepared for us to walk in. Help my parents, Lord, help white Charleston, help me to activate our concern for our fellow man, to walk in your good works. Thank you, Lord.

*

July 4. Though the center was closed for the holiday today, I decided to try to enlist some of the boys for camp anyway. Today, I figured I could probably catch the mothers at home, and the fathers too if any of these boys have fathers. All weekend I have been debating with myself whom I should take to camp. What criterion can I use to select six boys from the twelve or fifteen I've been working with? At first I thought it would be an easy decision to make. I could sit down and draw up a list of the "best" six boys, those who have worked the hardest on the clean-ups and shown the most interest in the activities. But then I remembered Lawrence, who would have been third or fourth on my list, Lawrence, whom the other boys call Teet. Pathetic Lawrence, whose teeth have rotted away leaving only little brown points on his gums. Lawrence, who smells of rotten teeth every time he speaks. Lawrence who wants to go to camp as much as anyone, even Doug.

The boys who normally go to this camp come from white middle- and upper-class families, a few from Charleston but most from small towns in the lower part of the state. The handful of other Negroes who will be there this summer will probably be from the most prominent Negro families in the state. And here I am — rounding up kids right from the heart of the ghetto. Shouldn't I at least pick the cleanest, the healthiest, the most intelligent ones I can find? If I take a boy like Teet — hell, that's apt to put an end to the camp for sure. But then why shouldn't I take him? He deserves to go; I know he'll have a great time, splashing in the water, sneaking out on the beach at night. . . .

I decided to pick someone else.

First on my list was Chief Panther Sneed, who's either

twelve or thirteen. He lives in a house that is cleaner on the outside than most. It's been painted white, not so long ago, with bright blue shutters. As I approached his place, I saw him with another boy catching baseball. He agreed to take me in to see his parents about camp. We go through the wire gate, held to the fence by a coat hanger, up the outside brick steps, and onto the porch, which tilts the opposite way from the house. He opens the door and walks briskly in. "Ain't you got no manners, boy?" comes a husky woman's voice from inside. "Why don't you knock before you enter?"

But this rebuke doesn't bother Sneed. "Come on, Mr. Barnwell."

"Are you sure it's all right?"

"Sho', man, come on in."

I enter a very dark hall, empty of everything except Sneed and me. A door on the left is open and reveals an entire family sitting around, scowling at us. It was apparently from this room that the voice yelled at Sneed. But we don't stop here; we go instead to a room at the back of the hall. This room, a porch, and another room is Sneed's home.

The room is dark. Sneed's mother is sitting on a sofa, which twenty years ago probably sat in the living room of one of Charleston's finest homes. The once resplendent colors are now a "nigger town" brown. His father is sitting next to her on a wooden chair, its back broken off. Even though this is the first time I've been in a Negro home since I tried to collect money on a bad bank loan I once made, I do not notice the rest of the furniture. I suppose there were many things in the room, pots and pans, a wood stove, boxes, tables, a radio; but it's so dark and drab in this room that there seems to be little distinction among the stuff that fills it. Even Sneed's mother and father blend into the darkness. They look at me as I enter, saying nothing, showing no awareness that I'm in the room except for the fact that they follow me with their eyes.

"May I sit down?" I ask. The man nods, ever so slightly. The woman remains completely motionless. I begin by remarking on how hot it is today. I start to say something funny but think better of it. Then I talk and talk about the camp, how it costs $50.00, but how we can pay most if not all of it, how the camp has recently been integrated though there should be no trouble in that respect, how I can drive Sneed there and bring him back. My words seem to evoke no response, so I stop and ask, "Do you think there's a chance Sneed can go?"

"I ain' know. How much you say he was?" Sneed's father is speaking.

"Fifty dollars, but you just tell me how much you can pay and let me worry about the rest."

Gradually this quiet man, who could be thirty-five or sixty-five, begins to talk. I watch his heavy moustache go up and down as he asks me several times to repeat where we are going, for how long, how much it will be. There is no response at all to my statement that Sneed would be going to an integrated camp. Is race too embarrassing to discuss? Is it not worth discussing? Have I made it clear that the camp is integrated?

Finally, Sneed's father says he can raise not five but ten dollars, and that he will let his son go to camp. After he signs his name, Luther Woodward, on the application, a long and painful process, I smile, thank the Woodwards for their time, and walk backwards to the door. It's exactly as it was when I entered the room, no response to my leaving other than a nod.

ever so slight. Once again Sneed's parents become part of the darkness and the mystery of that room.

Outside, the sunlight was blinding. I got Sneed to show me where some of the others on my list live, and saw three more parents before I concluded that I was trying to be some kind of a martyr by working on the Fourth of July.

July 5. Today, I visited the mothers of the two other boys on my list for camp. Luckily, they were both home. All of the calls were difficult. No one wants to trust me. Perhaps the call on Doug's mother was the hardest. When I went to see her this morning, she was sitting on a chair in the middle of the doorway to her small home, tremendously fat, a stocking wrapped around the top of her head, queen of her domain. I approached.

"Well, good morning, Mrs. Duncan, my name is William Barnwell. I'm a seminarian and I've been working with . . ."

"What you want from me, white boy?"

"Ma'am, I don't want anything from you. I want to see about taking . . ."

"Go 'way from here. I ain't interested."

"Didn't Doug tell you about going to camp?"

"So you's the one got him all stirred up 'bout camp? Well, I ain' lettin' him go. He's spent all his money."

And we talked and we negotiated and we talked some more. Finally, right when I was ready to give up on Doug's mother, she reached down in the bosom of her dress and pulled out a five-dollar bill. "Now I ain' 'bout to send that boy for nuttin'." She handed me the bill, raised her head high, frowned once again, indicating that she was really ready for me to leave this time. I did.

I told Father Andrews that I had gotten six boys to sign up for camp, Sneed, Doug, William, Allen, Jerome, and Champ, but that I had not been able to enlist any girls for their camp session. And today was the last day that the diocese would accept applications. I expected him to be irritated about my missing out on the girls, even though I had tried to recruit some of them. But instead of being mad, Father Andrews was surprised that I got *any* of the boys' parents to agree. Well, how about that, I thought to myself, I've scored a victory.

The Boys Club meeting was successful today. I gave them some Scout instructions, then boxing lessons, then took them into the chapel to explain the difference between Jesus and us. Adam told me at our staff meeting that Father Andrews is pleased with my work but hinted that both he and Father Andrews are worried that I'm "going too soft on the boys." In the month of August, Father Andrews will be on vacation and I'll be in charge. I must establish an authoritative image by then. There will be no Father Andrews to run to.

Coming out of Mr. Dick's, I almost bumped into Teet, who had evidently been waiting on me. "My mother's home now, Mr. Barnwell. You can come talk to her about the camp."

"Sorry, Lawrence," I said, looking away from him, "we're all filled up. I'm really awfully sorry, fellow, but we can only take six this year. Maybe next year."

Lawrence argued for a while, though I'm sure he knew it was futile. And why did I have to lie about "next year"?

*

July 6. I feel like quitting. I believe I would except for two reasons: one, I can't quit because I'm under obligation to the diocese; two, I can't quit because I've told everyone in town how important this work is. And after Sunday's entry, I'd look mighty stupid if I gave it all up now.

On days like today I begin to believe what some of my night world people have been saying all along — "Those Nigras don't want help" — you are supposed to say that slowly as you pound your fist on the table. They want no change. In their own way, they are just as conservative as the whites who live on the other side of town. Or perhaps "apathetic" and "irresponsible" are better words. The sewing class doesn't want to sew. Sally is legitimately furious at Adam for not having swept the center decently in a week. "It'll do these Head Start children more harm than good if they have to come and play in filth." Father Andrews has apparently given Sally little support in such matters. Today, the boys killed my favorable image of the Boys Club. Instead of trying to start fires with the sticks, they threw them at each other and pretended that they were cigarettes. In the boxing class, they didn't want instructions, they wanted to box their own way. And ever since the Bible School terminated, the worship services, which I've held in the afternoons, have generally been failures. The few boys and girls that I've coaxed into the chapel haven't wanted to worship. It interferes with the games they play when I have my eyes closed in prayer. Rather than better ourselves, they seem to say, let's leave things the way they are, chaotic.

But what got me especially down was Sneed's mother. Her husband had promised to bring me ten dollars today toward the camp fee. At five o'clock, when it was clear that no money would be forthcoming, I called on Mrs. Woodward. She met me at the outside door this time and talked to me through the screen. "We ain' lettin' Sneed go." She sounded irritated.

"Is there anything I can do to help?" I asked. "As you know, we can give even more money toward the camp."

"No, we ain' lettin' him go and that's that."

I couldn't think of anything to say but "Thanks, anyway" as I smiled meekly and walked away. And that was that. It was too late to sign up another boy in Sneed's place.

Now why wouldn't Sneed's parents let him go to camp? And why did Mrs. Woodward have to be so uncompromising and rude about it? If I were arguing with a segregationist, I'd probably answer these questions by saying that for generations the Negro couldn't trust the white man to help him. . . . And why were they so inconsiderate as to prevent some other boy from going in Sneed's place. . . . When a slick young fellow comes talking about a white children's camp, these folks naturally run him off. I must have seemed to the Wood-wards not much different from certain life insurance, vacuum cleaner, and graveyard plot salesmen, who suck every drop of blood out of the Negroes.

But today, I don't look on things that way. Besides being startled by Mrs. Woodward's rudeness, I think she is flat wrong in stopping her son from going to camp, wrong and not excusable. Not only would Sneed be in an integrated situation for the first time in his life, and have a chance to see what life in his country can be like; but he would also take part in well-organized activities and have a lot of fun. Mrs. Woodward seems to reject the camp simply because it is something new, and because what is new is never good. How are we going to get these people to push forward, to risk change?

If it is arrogance that white Charleston must overcome in

order to be able to see life through the Negro's eyes, the problem the Negro must overcome is apathy and irresponsibility. This is my first encounter with Negroes and a white camp; but in the course of my life, I reckon I've heard a thousand stories about how in other connections Nigras are lazy and no good. So-and-so, the sexton, at such-and-such a church never does anything but drink all the Communion wine. Old Doctor Jones, the gardener, is a happy and good-natured fellow, but he ain't worth a damn. And Rosemary gets drunk so often that she is totally unreliable; why she even dropped the turkey in the middle of the dining room floor one Christmas. In recent years, I've been accusing friends and family of exaggerating, of allowing their prejudice to blind their eyes. But after today, hell, I just don't know.

I am still mad and still feel like quitting, but now, as I vomit up my anger on the typewritten page and as I'm cooled off by my parents' attic fan breeze, things begin to look somewhat better. Now I can say this much, "The very reason I feel like quitting is what makes this work so important."

July 7. The diocese couldn't find me a place to take the boys and girls on all-day trips. Father Andrews did. He has a Negro friend who owns a lot on the water some fifty miles south of Charleston. It was there that I took the Wildcats today. All were present, except Teet. Timothy and Black-y-mo tried to fight their way into the car, but they are too young to be Wildcats. We were in good spirits as we drove away from the center, the boys because they were going crabbing and were going to cook out, me because we were going to a place where we would be genuinely welcomed, not to a family estate owned by some nervous white person who might let us picnic on his place but only reluctantly.

The trip down was through some of the prettiest country anywhere, under the tunnels that the ancient moss-covered oak trees make over the road, by the banks of saltwater rivers, over wooden bridges that creak exactly as they did in the horse-and-buggy days. And then there we were at the friend's place, Jordan's Paradise Acres. There are a few pink flamingos standing up in the front yard, not showing too much rust, numerous cook-out grills in the backyard, covered with rust. The little house on the place is box-shaped, painted white, and looks like any other box-shaped house. And the oaks on the lot are as pretty as any. And the river behind is wide; its clear blue color provides a perfect contrast to the green marsh on either side of it.

Sneed insisted that before we put out the crab lines, we leave the meat in the sun a little while "so's it will stink up real good." And since Sneed is the patrol leader, that's exactly what we did. While waiting for the stink to start, we lit the fire, using seventy-six matches. Then the boys asked me if they could go swimming. I wouldn't let them all go at once, but I did agree to take them one at a time.

The first boy in split his foot open on an oyster shell. When you have been raised on the water in this part of the state, you learn from an early age how to walk on oyster shells as you make your way from the bank to the deeper water. The trick is to step very carefully and lightly, and as soon as you get into water about knee-deep, you begin shifting your weight from your feet, making use of the buoyancy of the water. That way, you only get slit toes, never anything serious. I made it to the deep water from the bank without a scratch. Then came William, an eleven-year-old boy who is no larger than my six-year-old nephew. He charged into the water like he was running to first base. I closed my eyes. Is the boy nuts? Doesn't he know what he'll do to his feet? Hasn't he been raised on the water in the Carolina lowcountry, same as me?

"William, did you cut your foot?"

"Ya suh."

"Is it bad?"

"Ya suh."

"William, is it real bad?"

"Ya suh."

I helped William out the water. Sure 'nuff, he had an inch-long gash in the upper part of his foot. Damn the segregated system that keeps my boys from knowing how to walk on oyster shells and keeps me oblivious to the fact that some of them have never seen an oyster shell bank in their lives.

I bandaged William's foot, demonstrating to the rest of the fellows how a Boy Scout must be prepared. Since William's foot was not bleeding now and he was in no pain, we went ahead with the outing. The boys caught twenty crabs, some kind of a record, and then sat down to the meal of black and raw hamburgers and corn that I cooked for them. Three Negro men walked up from down the road while we were eating, said "Good morning," and then proceeded to bail out a half-sunk rowboat, one that was so deteriorated that I thought it had been abandoned. But these men squeezed in and, with one paddle, shoved off into the strong current in pursuit of catfish and croaker. I am positive they had to wait for the tide to change before they returned, if they returned. I doubt if they know much more about the water than William. It's Negroes like those who keep the number of drownings each year so high in this part of the country.

After dinner, the boys filled a rusty old kettle that they found in the backyard with salt water and boiled the twenty crabs over the fire. They ate every part of every crab, except for the outside shell and the "dead man" inside. About three-thirty, we left after the usual fight to get them to pick up the trash they had thrown everywhere.

William's mother was out looking for a job when we returned to Charleston, so I decided to take him to the hospital myself. But before we could go, he had to show his cut to Linda. I guess, since I've been at the center, thirty children have taken their cuts and bruises to Linda to bandage up and make over. William said that he'd never been to a doctor before, but after seeing the "nice nurse lady in the emergency room" he showed no more fear. The guy that took the information at the hospital didn't want to believe William was eleven and that he spelled his last name, sometimes with an "s" and sometimes with a "z." But the white nurses there all took a liking to William and they referred to him as that "cute little fellow."

Waiting outside while they sewed up William, I struck up a conversation with a young Negro man who was waiting for his wife and baby. He said that his name was Frank and that he had recently completed his college education up north. He is one of the few Negroes in town who hold clerical jobs. Frank told me about the present racial situation in Charleston from his point of view. He is amazed by the progress this city has made, by the fact that decent jobs are beginning to open up, by the fact that you can eat most anywhere you want to, though sometimes you do get scowled at, by the fact that the schools are becoming more integrated each year. He said, however, that he thought we had a long way to go. I'm afraid he doesn't know how far. He could not tell me why the Negroes so seldom use their recently earned "privileges" of eating in restaurants, of going to the movies. I told him that I was glad he had come back South, because too many Negroes of his caliber and education are staying away. "Well," he said, "it sure was a lot easier for me up there. But after all, this is home."

Frank is the first Negro with whom I've talked about the racial situation this summer. We belong to the same generation, we were both raised in Charleston, we have both lived away for a time. We speak the same language. Adam shows no interest in talking race. And I still feel awkward around Father Andrews. He's quite friendly now and seems glad to have me working at the center. Why can't I open up with him as I did with Frank? Am I afraid that once I start talking race he'll have me going to civil rights meetings and integrated parties? Do I have an authority problem with him? Do I secretly not want to "lower" myself to talk intimately with Father Andrews? Hell, I just don't know.

William had five stitches in his foot and probably more attention paid him than ever before in his life. Afterward, I took him out and bought him a milk shake and a hamburger, then delivered him home to his mother. On seeing her, he proudly exhibited his bandaged foot and told her that he didn't cry a bit. Of all the Wildcats, William enjoyed the picnic the most.

*

July 8. For the second day running, the temperature has risen to ninety-seven degrees. Fortunately, we were today able to set up the above-the-ground swimming pool, the largest that Sears carries. It was bought for some white kid downtown, never used, and given to us after a year of going empty. Children from blocks around came to play in it.

Richard followed me most of the morning, tugging on my shirt, until, finally, I took him into the storeroom to find a bathing suit. He'd pull out some fat man's pajama bottoms and hold them up, asking me in his own way if they'd do for a bathing suit. I would shake my head, no. Then he'd grab a piece of lace underwear and hold it up. "No, Richard." And then something else. Finally, he scooped up a handful of sweeping compound and threw it all over the old clothes and all over me. Whereupon, I took him to the dime store and bought him a bathing suit. They say Richard never showed any signs of intelligence until the seminarian who worked at the center last summer started paying him some attention. My predecessor would have been proud of his boy Richard today.

Within a few minutes after I had turned the children loose in the fifteen-foot pool, the water was filthy. But since everyone was having such a good time, I just tripled the amount of chlorine rather than run them out.

About five in the afternoon, Father Andrews and I were shooting pool and waiting for the rest of the day to pass when who should appear at the front door of the center but my old fishing buddy John. John is the most conservative South Carolinian I know. He's so well known as conservative, in fact, that he doesn't have to do anything to prove it any more. John is from a medium-sized town in the lowcountry. He's the grandson of a wealthy planter, the son of an alcoholic home — both parents now dead, one a suicide — himself a nervous wreck. If he were from Charleston, he would be considered a "character." He has no idea what he wants in life. One day he sells insurance, the next he plants cotton, the next he enlists in the service — in fact, that's where I met him several years ago. The next day he has found a way out of the service and has flown to Hawaii to spend a year but is back home again in two weeks. He dates many good-looking girls but does not seem able to settle on any one of them. John is the dream hero of the "Southern" novelist. Life is hell for him, but he remembers a time when the South was rich and magnificent, when hundreds of slaves planted and harvested crops on his ancestors' place, a time when Francis Marion gallantly drove the English crazy. It is this memory of a golden age that keeps John going. A time when South Carolina was a leading state, economically and culturally.

When we first met in the service, John and I would argue to the point of fighting. But those were the days before he became too conservative even for the John Birch Society and before I went to seminary. Now, neither of us takes the other seriously, at least most of the time. I call him Swamp Fox, he calls me Wild William. But on seeing John's bright red face and wavy blond hair, in the middle of the mission center doorway, I was — today — most serious. "Good to see you, Swamp Fox. What in the hell are you doing in Charleston?"

"Well, if it isn't the wild one himself." He was grinning. He then turned to Father Andrews, introduced himself, shook hands, and told us to finish our game. I was so nervous that I let Father Andrews come up from behind and win the game. You never know what to expect from John. Last year

he appeared one day at my seminary and gave one of the seminarians I introduced him to such a hard time that the boy used
John as a sermon illustration in the preaching class. When we
were in the service, John threw his Yankee roommate out of
the door on more than one occasion. His temper is so violent
that he fights, he shouts, he even threatens to kill. And here
was Father Andrews, the symbol of the new order of things,
the educated and sophisticated Negro, beating me at pool.

After the game, I coaxed John away from my boss as soon as
I could and introduced him to some of the children throwing
horseshoes in the yard. John was at home with these kids. Actually, he's been around Negroes much more than I. Every
time we've been fishing together, he's taken along a colored
fellow he calls Napoleon. Napoleon, who's about our age and
who loves John, seems especially happy when John teases him.
But Napoleon knows his place, and it "ain't messin' round
with no Josephine." At only one point did I have to slow John
up. He was mimicking Black-y-mo's speech impediment and
he went too far and scared the little boy. My strategy in intro-
ducing John to the children was to stall for time. I know that
he can't do any one thing for more than a few minutes and I
figured that he'd soon get bored and leave. I was wrong. He
said to me, "You know, I believe I'll go talk to Father What's-
his-name for a while; he seems like an interesting fellow."

Interesting fellow. What in the hell did he mean by that? I
followed John inside, clasping my hands as if in prayer. A representative of the past meets a representative of the future, my
night world meets my day world. I lingered behind. I didn't
want to see my two worlds destroy each other, didn't want to
be the one to witness God's first-day creation changed back to
the primordial *tohu vabohu*. But not John, he walked straight

up to Father Andrews. I heard him say, "Father, something's been on my mind for a long time. I'd like to ask you about it." Here it comes. I picked up the pool cue, nervously. Would that question be, "What do you think of Martin Luther King?" Or, "How come the Nigras in the South go places where they aren't wanted?" Or, what would it be? I almost crawled under the pool table in shame for having underestimated both John and Father Andrews when I heard the discussion that followed. The question that had been on John's mind for a long time was this, "Father, do you believe that God is dead?"

Father Andrews counseled John for half an hour or more on how God is alive, as much as ever, though we often become dead in our ways to him. I stood aside, tapping the pool cue on the floor with one hand, covering up my mouth with the other, every bit as puzzled by John as my seminarian friend had been. It occurred to me in the course of the conversation that I had never discussed religion with Father Andrews, never asked for his help. And here was John, Francis Marion the Swamp Fox reincarnated, absorbing everything this well-informed, sensitive Negro priest was saying.

At times like this, I forget about the tragedies of life, the apathy of the ghetto, the arrogance of the white South, and say to myself, "Life's not tragic; life's a comedy. It's crazy, man!"

July 10. The church where Father Andrews holds services on Sunday looks deserted. High weeds have grown up around it, mortar from the brick walls is crumbling away, there is no sign or marking to indicate that the building is an Episcopal church.

My wife and I found our way to the church this morning only because we recognized Father Andrews's car outside.

We were somewhat nervous about going to his church. In the first place, the church is in a white neighborhood; in the second, since it draws on an entirely different crowd from the mission center, we didn't know anyone in the congregation. Is this where all those militant civil rights people that I expected to find this summer have been hiding? Would the Negroes welcome us in their church? Or, would they tell us to go back to St. Thomas'? And what about the white neighbors, would they dub us a couple of half-beat agitators? Taking my wife to Father Andrews's church was a little like jumping into the water. I really had no choice about it. He will be away on vacation in August and, since I will have to preach in this church twice, I must find out something about it.

Our fears were not alleviated when the woman who met us at the door almost turned white with surprise on seeing us there. (I haven't learned to say "lady" yet and am not sure of value of that word anyway.) The service began. "The Lord is in his holy temple, let all the earth keep silence before him." Then the Confession, then the Absolution, then the Lord's Prayer. Recently, I have been very critical of our liturgy, which I find stereotyped and difficult to understand. Today, however, I rejoiced in the fact that I am an Episcopalian and will always have in common with everyone in my denomination the same service. My wife and I were light years away from these people, in so many ways we were strangers; but we did share with them the same form of worship. When we reached the Psalm, I was feeling warmly toward the women in bright-colored dresses sitting in the next row and toward two children on the right, who were rolling coins on the floor and ducking the swats of their older sister.

In fact, I was put so much at ease by the familiar service and the people of Father Andrews's church that by the time we reached the Second Lesson, I was dreaming again, thinking of the fancy cocktail and supper club some friends had taken us to last night. It's one of the places where the young, well-born Broad Street businessmen and their wives hang out. Though some of the older crowd still comes, most of the people you see there are in their thirties. Once again I talked about race and ghettos and white responsibility all night. My wife says I'm getting to be a "real bore."

While we said the Creed, prayed for peace, grace, and all the conditions of men, I was reliving my conversations of last night. To a fat and happy salesman, who talks too much but is still good company, almost a "character" himself, who had asked me what I was doing with the niggers this summer, I answered "Stirring them up to give the idle rich like yourself something to fuss about." To my descriptions, he answered, "Well, just don't give me anything to shoot at."

To perhaps the most liberal businessman on Broad Street, a man who delights in shocking people with his unpopular views on race and politics, but a man, nevertheless, who is one of the few citizens in Charleston seriously trying to respond positively to this changing world, "I know you've been going around scaring old ladies and drinking buddies with your views, but what have you actually *done* about the travesty of justice in our city?" I was needling. To me, "Not a damn thing. I don't know where to begin. I go uptown and talk to some of the people in the slums, but I can't understand what they are saying, much less what they seem to need." A man who has made his stand, strong and unambiguous, and a man more modest than I.

To one of the older men, some sort of executive, who had just told four or five of us standing around him that he hopes they get their craw full of it in Chicago, "Their craw full of what?" To me, "Niggers, goddam niggers, that's what." Then to his wife a little later who told me how terrified she was of the colored people in Charleston who stole from and beat up the whites, "Well, what are you going to do about it?" To me, "Why, I'm going to send the maid home in a taxi."

The grace of our Lord Jesus Christ, the love of God, and the fellowship of the Holy Ghost. The sermon appropriately enough was on doing positive things rather than merely abstaining from doing wrong things. The children on the right were looking for God up in the ceiling now. The congregation seemed attentive. When the sermon was about over, another seven or eight people came into the church, but their tardiness didn't seem to bother the preacher. Then we sang an Episcopal hymn, which somewhat hampered these folks' expressiveness but was nevertheless moving.

After the worship was over, we stood in something like a receiving line at the door with Father Andrews and met everyone. Friendly people! One ancient woman with an old Charleston name, as familiar as the names of any of those at the club last night, a woman who has probably partially dominated and been loved by some white family she's been with for fifty years, came up to us and spoke as though she were talking to a close friend she hadn't seen in years. "I sho' am glad you folks came here dis morning." She took my hand and held it with both of hers. "Please come back again." Niggers, goddam niggers, that's what. All day I've been trying, without success, to sing that Episcopal hymn the same way they did.

July 11. I thought my day was going to turn out to be a dull one; but beginning in the early afternoon, I found out differently. First, I had a long talk with an old fool, a poor old Negro man who smiles all the time, showing his front teeth that are still white but whittled away until they look like fangs. Then I was unexpectedly invited to attend the mission center board meeting and had another long talk with some of the elite and most civic-minded of Charleston's white business world. The foolish and the wise — both in one afternoon.

The fool is short and slouches. He was clean and neatly dressed except for one shoelace that was untied. When he introduced himself to me as "Freddie," he looked the other way as he spoke. "I hear'd 'bout your Boy Scout troop, and I come to look on your meetin' dis afternoon, if dat's okay wit' you."

"Certainly, is there any particular reason why you're interested?" I wasn't paying much attention.

"Well, suh, you see I'm looking for a Scout troop meself as mine ain' goin' no more."

A scoutmaster? This fellow? Good God, I hope we aren't that hard up. "Sure, what happened to your troop?"

He straightened up and spoke slowly. "I have produce many good Scout. I have risen from assistant scoutmaster to full scoutmaster. But now all the boys are too old and I have no more Scouts."

I'd like to see some of those "good Scouts" this guy has produced. "Tell me about yourself, sir." I was paying more attention now. Freddie told me that he has a heart condition or, in his words, "high blood," and is not able to work. And Freddie said that when he's not in bed he spends his time forming groups of boys and girls to keep them off the streets and interested in something worthwhile. Besides working with the Boy Scouts in the afternoons, he has also started model airplane clubs in the mornings for the smaller children and a large organization for the "young ladies and gentlemans" in high school that meets three nights a week and is called the Young American Citizens. It is about this latter organization that we first talked. Freddie is pleased with the number of members he has — near sixty — but is worried that he can't answer all their questions. Some examples:

3. Why not bomb the Viet Cong like we did in the Philippines?
5. Why do the U.S. tell all the things she do?
9. If God wrote the Ten Commandments and they broke up when Moses got angry, who wrote them down the second time?

Those questions and others were neatly written down on lined paper which Freddie stored in a shiny brown briefcase, on which were his initials, engraved in gold.

Then he showed me some of the things he had composed for his young people to read. I couldn't make out much of what was there. Not only was it mostly illegible, but Freddie had also sounded out the words to spell them. I did recognize one quotation. "Ax not what your cuntry can do for you, no, sir, ax what you can do for your cuntry." So this guy meets with young people and they decide how they can improve our country, whether or not we should bomb the Viet Cong like we did in the Philippines and whether or not Moses wrote the second set of commandments. Then he produced a document that he said he was most proud of, one that he had rewritten several times. I am positive that someone else either wrote it or had completely reworked the English, for it was grammatically correct. He let me copy it.

A Message to Young Americans

Do you know how fortunate you are to be living in a free land? You can come and go without reporting. You can worship God as you wish. As American citizens, we are proud that the U. S. is a leader of the free nations. It was bought at a great price by the men who founded this nation. Freedom is not cheap. It was defended on fields of battle by men who fought, and died that freedom might not perish. In a few short years, you who are young citizens today will take your place among those who are responsible for the national welfare.

How fortunate, how goddam fortunate!

After I was through with the Boys Club meeting — the most disorderly yet — I let Freddie talk to the fellows. They gathered around him like the disciples gathered around Jesus and listened to every word he said. Here is some of what followed:

"And what you do when a snake crawl in de tent?"

"Tell us, Mr. Freddie."

"Do you hit dat snake?"

"Lawd no, Mr. Freddie, you don't hit dat snake."

"Do you run from dat snake?"

Gulp. "No, Mr. Freddie, you don't even run from dat snake." The boys' eyes were getting big.

"I'll tell you what you do!"

"Oh, tell us, Mr. Freddie, tell us."

He looked around, squinting his eyes, at the boys one by one, like a detective on television the morning after the murder. "I'll tell you what you do. You close your eyes and you goes back to sleep."

"Oh, lawd no, Mr. Freddie!" The boys started to laugh.

Surprised at their unbelief — "Das right, man. Dat snake only come into yuh tent to get warm." The boys were quiet and serious once again. Freddie, raising his voice to a high pitch, "Let him crawl under the blanket with you and he'll leave you alone. Be nice to that snake and he'll be nice to you."

Now my eyes were getting big. Did this come from the Boy Scout manual or the Sermon on the Mount?

"And what happens when you bad? In my Scout troop. . . ."

"What happens, Mr. Freddie?"

"Boy, you ever hear of de belt line? Well, in my Scout troop, you goes through the belt line twice, once for disgracing your patrol, once for disgracing your troop. But you don't use the buckle in my troop." He was shaking his finger. Then Freddie talked about the Scout laws, told of a forty-mile hike he'd taken the boys on but how he had to give up "dem long walks on behalf of de high blood." Then he talked about the uniform and how a true Scout never lets it get dirty but always keeps it clean. He talked about doing a good turn daily, sweeping the center, helping old ladies across the street, doing what Mr. Barnwell tells them to do, picking up the trash in the neighborhood, and lastly about trying to find a way to keep the little children interested in doing something worthwhile and off the streets. The time passed quickly. The boys loved Freddie and made him promise to come back soon. I was bewildered by it all. How can this funny little man do "deese t'ings" when I can't?

Shortly after he left, the board members began arriving. The board consists of several of the most prominent Broad Street businessmen — their suits well tailored, their features distinguished — three of the most able men from the Negro community, a clergyman, and Sister Margaret, the Catholic nun whose mission center is a few blocks from us. What a collection of talent, I thought to myself as I met these people one by one. This must be the closest thing in the city to a bi-racial committee, though these people know better than to use such a title. I wonder who put this committee together. Here are leading white citizens, part of the segregated order, meeting leading Negro citizens to talk about improving the conditions of the slums. And these white people didn't need to go to seminary to respond in this way. Isn't this exactly what we are after?

The meeting was called to order by Father Andrews. The first half hour the white businessmen discussed the relationship between the government's poverty programs at the center and the religious life. There seems to have been much correspondence between the government, the board members, the diocese, and others about whether or not the religious life at the center violates the First Amendment rights of the children in Head Start. These men were well read and quite familiar with the Supreme Court decision regarding such matters. There were arguments for and against. Though they were articulate and convincing, I was becoming uneasy and fidgety. I'm not thoroughly familiar with the church-state debate. I've never encountered this problem at the center and wasn't quite sure what they were talking about and why they were talking about it. The debate went back and forth. The Negroes looked as puzzled as I. Finally, Sister Margaret brought it to a close when she said, "Well, gentlemen, let me tell you how it goes in practice. The other day we were singing prayers before lunch at our place when the government inspector arrived to check on our anti-poverty program. He said to me, 'Sister Margaret, next time you see me coming when you are having grace, please tell me to inspect the playground facilities outside, and then you'll be happy and I'll be happy.' " Everyone laughed.

Men of the quality of those who sit on our board are accustomed to meetings that last one hour, no more. Thirty minutes were gone. For the next order of business, one of the white members brought up the point that we should get the parents of the youth in the neighborhood involved with the work of the mission. "We help the parents' children," he said, "the parents help us. There is a mutual responsibility, which hopefully will mature into a wider civic responsibility." Isn't this exactly what the center should be working toward? Certainly, such a plan to generate neighborhood leadership could not be called paternalistic. The white man continued, "The people of this neighborhood could hold regular meetings here at the center. They could sponsor clean-up drives. They could meet here for neighborhood social activities." Everyone was nodding his head, except the Negroes and me.

"I like your idea, sir, in theory." I heard myself speaking for the first time. "But I've called on a lot of the parents and I don't really think it's possible to generate this kind of work from them. Many of the mothers work all day, have six to twelve children at home, have no men to help out." Then a

Negro who works professionally with delinquent Negro children spoke for the first time and backed me up, enthusiastically. But the board would have none of it. "Are you sure it's that they don't have time?" one of them asked. "Or is it lack of interest?" The white board members were making a valid point. There *is* more than merely time involved. You might call it lack of interest; I've called it apathy and irresponsibility, but that's not the whole story. This *thing* we were talking about is at least partially due to the ghetto Negro's complete lack of familiarity with and distrust of what the white man calls "civic responsibility." As the businessmen talked on and on about how we could organize, I was thinking of Sneed's parents, Doug's mother who wanted to know what that white seminarian boy who came to call wanted from her, and William's mother who had never taken him to a doctor. Finally, I said, "I agree with you in theory, your plan *is* anti-paternalistic, but really, I think we must start with the children, not the adults. If you don't believe me, come make some calls with me and I'll prove it to you."

No, that was my job, not theirs. Theirs is to manage the center as a board of directors, to help Father Andrews plan the budget and his activities, to see that repairs are made on the old church building, (such as the broken windowpane in the library where we were sitting). Like any good board of directors, their contact is with the management, not the rank and file. In the short time that remained for our meeting, they covered many items of business quickly and efficiently. They want to get us some recreation equipment and talked about the difference between heavy duty and extra-heavy duty swings. They want the center to look cleaner and talked about how each day the children who play in the center could take turns sweeping and mopping. The older boys with nothing to do could lead them. There was no response to my request that we get downtown people to take children out on picnics to their places in the country.

As they talked on, I was thinking of Brian. You will remember that he changed his mind about coaching boxing in this neighborhood — too drab. Now he sends me twice weekly, by mail, a typed list of things to do when I coach the boys, a list which takes no little time to make up. And then I was thinking about Freddie. And the Young American Citizens. And about snakes and "high blood." And about model airplanes "that really fly."

What shall we say of the foolish and the wise? What is going on this afternoon. Who is Freddie? Who are these people sitting here at the table in the library? Has all this happened before? He looked up and saw the rich putting in their gifts into the treasury; and he saw a poor widow put in two copper coins. And he said, "Truly I tell you, this poor widow has put in more than all of them; for they all contributed out of their abundance, but she out of her poverty put in all the living that she had." That's all I know to say. All the living he had.

Father Andrews, who had said almost nothing, closed the meeting with a prayer.

July 12. After a hard day's work of organizing, playing with the kids, and cleaning up, I returned home with colored food in my stomach, colored smell on my clothes, colored sweat on my body, tired but "feelin' fine."

*

July 13. This morning I walked over to Sister Margaret's Neighborhood House. We are planning to sponsor a joint folk song program for the youth of both neighborhoods next week. She has two seminarians working with her this summer who will do the strumming. Our conversation drifted to civil rights in Charleston. Sister Margaret must be one of the most involved white Roman Catholics in the movement here. She seems to know all the Negro leadership and has promised to introduce me around. In spite of the fact that I've worked a month among Negroes, I have yet to talk to any of the key figures in any of the civil rights organizations. Before I came to the center, I was worried that I would become too much associated with civil rights groups. Since arriving, I have wondered if there *is* any organized Negro movement here at all.

If there is, I want to meet its leaders, talk with them, find out what their objectives are, see how my work this summer and perhaps my lifetime work relates to theirs. At the present moment, I am of the opinion that there ought to be two distinct forces at work attempting to alleviate injustices directed toward the Negro.

First, there will have to be a movement that regards the white segregationist as an enemy to be defeated, a movement dominated by Negroes who have been in chains most of their life and who are now dedicated to defeating the man who suppresses them, the man who may or may not know what he's doing. It must not be controlled by well-meaning whites, like myself or my more liberal seminary colleagues who have never belonged to the persecuted brotherhood. This movement will sometimes demonstrate, will sometimes shout "Black Power," will sometimes tacitly ally with Communists and guys that carry knives. It will know that few bi-racial committees in the South will give Negroes what they really want. It will know that white gifts are not the solution anyway. There is one way for Negroes, especially ghetto Negroes, to get what's coming to them in this country and that is to stand up and fight for it themselves, exactly as the unions did, exactly as James Baldwin is doing now — Baldwin, who in *The Fire Next Time* wrote, "I was icily determined — even more determined, really, than I then knew — never to make my peace with the ghetto but to die and go to Hell before I would let any white man spit on me, before I would accept my 'place' in this republic." This movement must know that the God of the Negro is black, brown, or tan, that the skin of the Negro is holy.

Our only hope for the prevention of a major revolution in my lifetime is the success of a minor revolution now. If the ghetto Negro finds no outlet for his mounting frustrations, no fulfillment for his potential in life, nothing more than doorsteps, welfare checks, and hand-me-down clothes; if he continues to smile when he hates, walk away when he is jammed to the wall, he will explode some day in complete anarchy; the irrational instinct to kill and destroy will win possession of and dominate him; he will be the Zookies grown up, the four angry men in the automobile more courageous, the boys and men with something to do; he will, the ghetto Negro, possess the stuff that great revolutions are made of. The adjectives now applied to him in a place like Charleston — lazy, irresponsible, apathetic, no-good — will be replaced by others — savage, regimented, vicious, tyrannical. He will look for military, not merely doctrinal, allies outside of this country. And he will fight to the last man.

Fortunately, there is, in this republic, a Negro movement in which men stand up, "icily determined" to win what is theirs, a movement which is, at this point in history, still American, still rational. I have never knowingly met anyone from this wing of the civil rights organizations. I doubt if it is seriously represented in Charleston. But I, like all Southerners, know that there is such a movement. It is precisely *this* movement that has brought pressure on the white South, on this white nation for that matter, and has caused us to stop and evaluate how much the segregated order is worth to us. Are we willing to keep our children out of school? Are we willing to withdraw our local church from the historic church? Are we willing to isolate ourselves from our great country, our America? And finally, are we willing to let our hate for our fellowman possess and destroy us? It is the Baldwins and the Martin Luther Kings that make us pay a price for segregation that is so high that if we do pay it we will be left bankrupt. It is also these men who give the ghetto Negro a cause in life, a purpose to "be." They and their revolution are our hope.

Second, there must be a movement generated from among the whites, with help from Negroes like Father Andrews and Freddie, that will respond constructively to the militant Negro movement. This second movement cannot dominate the revolt. It may, in fact, have to remain *entirely* separate from it. One movement cannot really appreciate the other at the present time. One is driving, one is receiving; both are necessary. It is the receptive movement that will vote important civil rights legislation and money for poverty programs *after* the militants demonstrate, threaten, and generally put the fear of God into the nation. It is this movement that will, hopefully, bring about the desegregation of institutions *before* the trouble comes. But perhaps most important, it is this movement that will learn and teach others that the Negro, the ghetto Negro, is a man, fully a man, and only a man, like anyone else. It will respond to the Negro *as* a man, a fellowman. It is through this movement that whites will experience integration for themselves and will learn that, once in, the water's good. It is this movement that we who want to do more than give old clothes — yet cannot demonstrate in the streets — can identify with and commit ourselves to.

If there is no driving force, there will be no receiving force. If there is no receiving force, there will be no real victory for the militants. They will be like Napoleon and his men who fought fiercely and successfully all the way through Russia to Moscow. When they arrived at their destination ready to proclaim victory, they could find no one to surrender to them. Moscow was empty! Let us hope that when the Negroes finally achieve their victory, that the South, that Charleston, will not be empty.

Now, Baldwin, I'll tell *you* something. You and your people need me and others like me, and like Sally and Linda. And furthermore, you need the board of directors of this center, and you need ministers who preach sermons on love as activated concern. Sure, we'll make mistakes, plenty of them; but then you aren't infallible yourself. If there aren't enough of us around, you'll win, pal, but you'll lead your men victoriously into empty churches, empty and bankrupt business districts, empty schools, empty housing areas. Empty and desolate. After the fire, the long and cold winter will set in. The surviving whites will be hiding somewhere in distant suburbia, talking about goddam niggers one moment, chuckling to themselves the next, waiting for your collapse. And you there, alone, in a strange land. So you fight your battle, we'll fight ours. Either we both win, or we both lose.

These are my ideas on the civil rights struggle at the present time. Perhaps after talking to some of the people that Sister Margaret will introduce me to, I'll think differently. Perhaps not.

July 14. Last week I asked for an appointment with my minister, the same one who preached on love as activated concern. I wanted to talk over some of my ideas with him. He suggested that he come see me at St. Paul's, where I could speak of these ideas in the setting from which they came. This morning, when he arrived, I gave him a summary of my summer's work, my idea of what the core of the problem is, and the ways I think we — who cannot and will not demonstrate — might do something about it without falling into the trap of dead-end paternalism. He liked most of what I said and seemed willing to try and help. We decided that what we must do is to get a small group of people who are willing to sustain a lot of disappointment before they quit, get them together, introduce them to the children and staff of the center and help them find specific things to do with the Negro youth. We spoke of picnics, tutoring, driving classes, art classes. We planned to start small and, hopefully, to grow larger. I was thinking to myself that my minister is a good man. I know he's busy, but I hope he follows through on what he's said.

Just before he left, he said, "Say, could you use somebody on Saturday mornings to teach singing lessons to the children?"

"Sure, who?"

"Me," he said. Me — I like that word.

That discussion really put me in the mood for my work this morning. I played with several of Sally's drippy-nosed Head Start children, told Mrs. Martin some funny stories, won three games of Ping-Pong. I even brought myself to tell Father Andrews about my friend's refusal to let me take one carload of kids to his place in the country — and I listened to him when he advised me not to let a chip develop on my shoulder. The Boys Club this afternoon was the best one so far. While Adam and I were drinking our late afternoon beer, he told me what a good job he and Father Andrews thought I was doing at the center. We talked and talked about my accomplishments. A perfect ending to a perfect day, I thought; there's nothing like praise. Not only have I got the racial problem solved intellectually but also I'm helping to solve it practically. Adam and I were getting so chummy that I suggested we have another beer. A fine idea.

About halfway through this one, he said, "You know, there is one thing I wish you'd do."

"Sure, what's that?" I was very interested and eager to listen to what this young man had to tell me.

"Command more respect from the fellows at the center."

Gulp. "How do you mean?" I knew exactly what he meant.

"Well, like at chapel the other day, those boys started cutting up, and you walked out. Don't *ever* walk out of the chapel in the middle of a service. Make them respect you so they will act right in chapel."

Adam was firm and strong. Suddenly, I felt like Mr. Dick's pickled pig's feet. He didn't even know the whole story. When I walked out, I said to the group, "If you don't have any more respect for God than this, it does more harm than good to have a worship service." I may have fooled some of the young people with this statement. One boy, in fact, after the service, came up to me, addressed me as "Father," and asked me please to forgive him. But not Adam — he'd have known who that God is I was speaking of.

"You're right about that, Adam," I heard myself saying. "I appreciate your telling me." I was lying of course; but since I smiled, Adam continued.

"And when those fellows cut up at the center, start picking on the little boys and throwing cards around, you know what I mean" — I did — "you've got to throw them out. When Father Andrews leaves, you're going to be in charge and, starting *now*, you've got to make them respect you."

Damn it. What do you mean? It's none of your business anyway. I'm second in command at the center and I'm the one who knows about worship. "Why yes, Adam, I believe you're right, I will have to crack down. I'll start tomorrow. It's very helpful for you to tell me these things." Damn your observations. Why do you, a Negro, who never finished the eleventh grade, have to be the one to uncover me and my shortcomings? You've tricked me, Adam.

He didn't stop with commanding respect; he told me everything that he saw wrong with me and everything that the fellows, young and old, at the center saw wrong with me. I smiled through it all, nodding my head in agreement. . . . Then came home and raised hell with my wife. . . . And she with me.

V

There's a Time for Dying

"You talk about precedent" — I was speaking softly — "about the future. What in the hell does that mean? I'm thinking about my boys right now and how society is *crucifying* them — without even knowing it."

"Crucifying? What do you. . . ."

". . . I love these boys, I believe in them." (I was bent over, beating my fist in my hand.) "I love them and society is crucifying them. My *Charleston* that I also love is crucifying them. It tears me apart. RIPS ME IN TWO. God help me.

"Goddammit.

"God help me. Goddammit.

"Goddammit. Goddammit. . . ."

"And he thinks he's going to be a minister of the church," a voice said from the next room.

My God, my God, why has thou for-
saken me?
Why art thou so far from helping me,
from the words of my groaning?
O my God, I cry by day, but thou dost
not answer;
and by night, but find no rest. . . .

For he has not despised or abhorred
the affliction of the afflicted;
and he has not hid his face from him,
but has heard, when he cried to him.

— Psalm 22

JULY 15. Sometimes I think I tremble too much. Twice to-day I got too emotional. The first time, I became so angry at a receiving clerk in the hospital that I couldn't hold the pen steady while I wrote a check. The second time, I had been talking calmly with my mother about race when I suddenly realized that I was shouting, crying, and shaking all over. My wife and mother worry about me when I lose control as I did today.

The trouble at the hospital was over whether or not William should have the stitches in his foot taken out there. Last week, the doctor told me to bring William back today and the stitches would be removed. Apparently, there is a fight of long standing between certain receiving clerks and certain doctors and nurses, for as soon as I mentioned what the doctor told me to do, the woman who was behind the window got furious. "We don't do follow-up work here. That's done at the clinic."

"But the doctor himself told me to bring this young fellow back. He's supposed to go to camp next Tuesday, and I won't have a chance to take him to the clinic."

"Why should we take out his stitches here? We never get paid in these cases. And there's the clinic. . . ."

"You never get paid? I had them bill the Episcopal Church for William. You'll get paid."

"Well, the bill went out last week, and we haven't gotten paid yet."

"How 'bout just taking out the stitches, Lady, you know very well that you'll get paid."

"Why should the Episcopal Church have to pay this bill? Tell me that. Do you know that this boy's father is a long-shoreman and makes $120 a week? You take him to his father and let *him* bring the boy in."

"Now, listen closely, Lady, this boy was hurt under my su-pervision and I'm bringing him in. You may know how much his father makes. *I* know that William has never been to a doctor in his life. If he really has a father as you say, he may not bring William in at all; and I don't want to take that chance. Do you know how these kids generally get rid of their stitches? They pull them out themselves. How'd you like your son to pull out his own stitches? You. . . ."

"We aren't going to take out the stitches, *Mister* Barnwell. The kind of work you seem to be doing is fine, and all like that, but there is a limit to everything. You can't march in here and make demands. William was treated for his cut, wasn't he? Given the care anyone else would have been given, wasn't he?"

"Now, listen, I'm sick and tired of people fighting out their political and personal battles at the expense of little children. It's none of your business who pays the bill, and you know it, and I know it. Since the church hasn't paid the bill yet and you seem to be able to hold that over me, I'll pay it myself." I couldn't take much more of this argument. My voice was be-coming higher and higher in pitch.

Clayton, the medical resident, the ex-member of the White Citizens Council, walked up and heard the last part of this conversation. "William," he said, "if you run into any trouble, let me know. I'm right here."

"Thanks," I said, surprised to see Clayton, "but everything is going to be all right."

I got out the checkbook and with great effort and pain wrote out the check for William's expense, eight dollars. The clerk who, in her self-assured calmness, must have been enjoying my awkwardness, took the check, turned away abruptly, as any lady would have done, and got another clerk to process the case.

We had started off arguing because of some minor office conflict, but we ended up arguing race. She knew that I represented something that she doesn't like. And I knew about her too. In Linda's words, "She wanted that nigger to pay his own bill," and nothing was going to stand in her way. Nothing, that is, but my conservative doctor friend Clayton.

I am gradually learning to keep control over myself in racial discussions and arguments, as I did the other night with the man and his crawful of niggers. But I find it much easier to keep my head when I'm talking about theories and movements and far-off places like Chicago than when I'm talking about specific situations with specific people in mind. William, who was completely puzzled by all this hot temper, was standing there by my side. By my side. I believe in that boy. In a way, I love him. And I'm not going to put up with it when some white lady tries to take out her anxieties on him, William, the most innocent one of all.

I calmed down, thought I had worked through my intense emotional feelings, went home, and was dumb enough to get in a discussion with my mother about why my friend had not let me take one carload of boys to his place in the country. "I see his point," my mother said. "He's worrying about setting a precedent. If he lets some in, more are apt to come back later, adults as well as children, and who knows, the place may be overrun with 'em." She was imagining herself living on the place in the country, looking across the field from the back porch of the house and seeing fifty noisy adult Negroes, drinking, "carrying on."

I was thinking of myself with the Panther Patrol today, out in the backwoods, at a new place I've discovered, a place not far from my friend's estate — thinking of how I watched the boys fish and crab, cook their own meal of hamburgers and corn in the shucks; of how I felt their trembling skin next to mine when I took them out into the deep water, one at a time, to teach them how to swim; of how I read the worship service to them under the tall pines and told them that Jesus would often go out to "a lonely place" to get away from the noise and confusion of city life.

"You talk about precedent," — I was speaking softly — "about the future. What in the hell does that mean? I'm thinking about my boys right now and how society is *crucifying* them — without even knowing it."

"Crucifying? What do you. . . ."

"Mother, if only you could have witnessed the absolute terror — and the love — of water these boys have, you'd know *exactly* what I mean. Mama, I love these boys, I believe in them." (I was bent over beating my fist in my hand.) "I love them and society is crucifying them. My *Charleston* that I also love is crucifying them. It tears me apart. RIPS ME IN TWO. God help me.

"Goddammit.

"God help me. Goddammit.

"Goddammit. Goddammit. . . ."

"And he thinks he's going to be a minister of the church," a voice said from the next room. It was then that I realized that I had lost control.

There's more than the trembling that bothers me when I lose control. I seem also to lose perspective, to make myself the measure of all things with no regard for anything, anyone else. In the two emotional outbreaks today, I did not think to question myself. I may have done the same thing, especially in the first situation, but I should have asked myself this question, "Are you so concerned because of the love that you have for these boys, or are you concerned that you yourself feel insulted or unheard?"

When the Archbishop of Canterbury, William Temple, said that revelation is the coincidence of divine event, which is external to man, and appreciation by individual man, he expressed concisely the ground of my theology, theology which I forgot today. Revelation, defined as The Truth, At-Oneness with God, or Perfect Fulfillment, is two-sided. One side starts with God outside of the individual man and is mediated to man through people, people living today, people living throughout history. The other side begins with the individual, who must respond to the external event, to *other* people, in his own way. Martin Luther made such an impact on the world because he understood revelation in the same way Temple did — except with him it was probably more of a "collision" of event and appreciation than a "coincidence." Luther knew the external event and he said, "Let God be God"; he appreciated it personally and he said, "Here *I* stand."

So if man is to be at one with The Truth, with God, or with himself, however he expresses it, he must listen to the people around him and to the people who lived before him. After listening and hearing others on *their* terms, the individual man accepts or rejects what he hears and then acts on it. If he accepts the word he hears, he tries to support it personally. He lives it. If he rejects the word he hears, he tries to attack and destroy it. In my emotional outbreaks today, I didn't listen to what was being said by the clerk or by my mother. I didn't want to face what was being said. I tried to cut off the clerk by writing a check to terminate an argument which was upsetting me. I tried to cut off my mother by screaming "Goddam" and walking out of the room. Only now at this typewriter am I beginning to appreciate the fact that my mother is upset not because of race but because of her concern for me, her son.

I lost my perspective when I lost my temper and thought only of myself and my own way. I ran. And I didn't listen to the voices of the past. Maybe they would have helped. Maybe if I had listened to what Jesus said about laying down your life for your friends, not for yourself. But I didn't do that — or anything close to that. And I'm paying for it now. I am not at one with myself, or God. I hate that woman because she was composed, and I was not. I hate myself because I have hurt my mother. I don't know — it's all so confusing.

July 16. No entry.

July 17. No entry.

July 18. All weekend I stayed confused, nervous, even sick at my stomach. A fishing trip with my father did not help. Neither did church. My realization that the events Friday were really not grave enough to bring on such depression only made the depression worse. This morning I could not sit down and plan the rest of the day as I usually do in the early morning. I thought about going home and going to bed, but I knew that whatever was bothering me would go to bed with me. The first thing I must do, I was thinking, is to calm down. How? I'm tired but can't sit still. I've been taking my work and myself too seriously. I'm sick of the whole works — night worlds, day worlds, everything. How *can* I shake it?

"Mr. Barnwell," said a very young voice, "can I hole de horseshoe?"

"Sure, Timothy, help yourself. Who you playing with?"

"I don't know. You want to play, suh?"

"You know, Timothy, I can't think of anything I'd rather do."

Eight-year-old Timothy with his horseshoe skill pulled me through this morning. Young David and his harp couldn't have done better. We played and played. My anxious mind was finally able to rest.

Later in the morning, I realized for the first time that Black-y-mo Edward had been in the same cowboy suit for at least three weeks. So I took him to the hand-me-down room to see what I could find for him, something he might wear for another three weeks. I found one near-perfect green shirt — only the armpit was torn — but no pants, no shoes. After he had put the shirt on with his cowboy pants, I turned him loose, thinking — well, that's better than nothing.

But Mrs. Martin, who had been watching us from the kitchen, caught Edward coming out of the door.

"Come here, boy!" she commanded. "I tell you what I want you to do." She opened her pocketbook and pulled out two soiled bills. "You take this money to your mother right now and tell her to get you a pair of pants and some tennis. You hear me, Edward! And don't come back to the center without them."

The fact that Edward returned in a couple of hours, exactly as he had left, with his mother two dollars richer, didn't matter so much.

It was almost time for lunch. Now, at long last, I was ready to get down to work. Several things had to be planned. The hootenanny which we are sponsoring jointly with the Catholics is to be Wednesday night. Linda and I are having an outing for the children under ten this Thursday. Tomorrow, I'm taking the five boys to the white camp. Last year I would have thought helping integrate a camp a most difficult task. Jumping in the water was hard, but this seems to be easy. And a week from tomorrow, the Boys Club is having a big dance for the high school youth.

After I had done my planning and eaten lunch, two white ladies arrived. They had heard all about the center and, judging from the conversation, have probably given some financial support to it.

"William," one of them said, "I think it's grand you are doing this kind of work."

"Thank you." I smiled. "I wanted to find out what goes on in the slums of our city, and this seemed to be the best way."

"You are so, so right. We've got to find out what goes on in all parts of Charleston, and do something about it. We're *too* proud of you."

"I appreciate your saying that. It helps to know that some people in Charlestown approve of me. I've heard that some don't."

We laughed a little.

"Don't worry about them. You keep up the good work. Now tell us exactly what you do here at St. Paul's."

After I had given them some of the details of my work, we smiled very pleasantly and said good-bye.

Barnwell, you've done it again! And after all that self-analysis over the weekend. Fellow, won't you ever learn? You've lapped up the praise and avoided the issue — you didn't cut people off this time; but, nevertheless, you have avoided possible criticism, possible pain. Why didn't you tell them about how little you are really doing? And about how you are taking five of these boys to the white camp tomorrow? And see what they would have said then.

No, I don't want to worry any more about my job. And no, I want the integration of the camp to be easy.

I had an ancestor who was once found by a policeman, quite drunk, in his tuxedo, on a garbage pile. When the policeman tried to help him up, my ancestor wouldn't let him. Staggering to his feet, slobbering all over himself, he said to the cop, "You leave me alone. Drunk or sober, I'm a gentleman and I refuse the help of *any* policeman." Drunk or sober, working on Broad Street or in the ghetto, we Charlestonians are gentlemen. We live by a certain code and probably always will as long as we are true Charlestonians. We like praise and we want to be left — alone.

Speaking of gentlemen, or rather "gentlemans," Freddie appeared this afternoon while we were having the Boys Club. He took charge right away and had the boys practice the

Scout laws, which somehow came out mixed up with the Ten Commandments. Then we talked about an overnight camping trip. Freddie knew of two places we could go. One, the well-known Skeeter Beach; the other, the marshy and shrubbery-covered land that has built up beneath the Cooper River Bridge as a result of harbor dredging. I envisioned broken jars and rusty beer cans.

"Tell you what, fellows," I said, "I'll look around myself and see if I can locate a place."

Freddie closed the meeting with a prayer to the Great Scoutmaster:

> Make us good Boy Scout.
> Keep us fed and clothed.
> Keep us off de corner.
> And forever respecting.
> For de Grea-a-a-a-a-at Scoutmaster's sake.
> Amen.

I continued the worship by taking everyone into the chapel. Following Adam's suggestions, I have been firm with the boys who cut up. This afternoon, I got Sneed and Goodie to act out a fight as I explained the text about turning the other cheek. I thought I had that passage figured out back at seminary, but if I did, I forgot its meaning today. By the time the sermonette was over, we all agreed that we weren't Jesus and, if someone hits you on one cheek, you'd better hit him back — quick. If only Freddie had stayed for the service! He'd have found a way out of that Biblical riddle.

July 19. After David had defeated and killed Saul, his one-time friend and king, he sang this song:

Thy glory, O Israel is slain upon thy
    high places!
  How are the mighty fallen!
Tell it not in Gath,
    publish it not in the streets of Ashkelon;
lest the daughters of the Philistines
    rejoice
lest the daughters of the uncircumcised
    exult. . . .

Saul and Jonathan, beloved and lovely!
  In life and in death they were not
      divided;
They were swifter than eagles,
    they were stronger than lions.

  Ye daughters of Israel, weep over Saul,
  who clothed you daintily in scarlet,
  who put ornaments of gold upon your apparel.

How are the mighty fallen
    in the midst of the battle.

It really takes very little courage to win a victory. But what
I saw this afternoon, the bravery I saw today, made me quietly
humble. Today was the day I took my five boys to help integrate the white church camp. All five were ready on time, at
two o'clock. Their mothers had gotten their things together
for them as I had asked and were there at the center to see
them off. As we drove away heading for the camp, which is
located some thirty miles south of Charleston on an island
that is windswept and deserted, I began giving instructions to
the fellows on how to take care of their clothes, how to brush
their teeth twice a day; then I told them not to worry about

the fact that the rest of the boys would probably be white. I guess I sounded apologetic about this last matter because Doug said to me, "Mr. Barnwell, we don't care 'bout de color of the skin, all we care about is the fun." And fun they will have. With that, I quit worrying about them.

It may require some courage for these fellows to mix with the fourteen white boys who signed up for the camp — but not much. The staff will look out for them, and they will look out for each other. Nor do I think it will take much courage for the white boys to get used to their first integration. They are young, under thirteen, and don't really worry much about things like this yet. After a couple of days, they will probably be having as much fun at camp as they had last year. The courage I saw today is mightier than the kind children are capable of, mightier than I'm capable of.

When we arrived at the camp, the staff had a table set up outside for registration. A laughingly pleasant girl, about eighteen, was sitting there with a couple of ministers and a woman who was evidently the dietitian. They were all amused when I told them that my boys were giving themselves nicknames that they had never used before. William, for example, told them his name was "Eggy." After they finished processing my gang, they sent them on with their bags to the building, a few hundred yards away, that they'd be staying in. I went along.

This building, which stands at the far end of the camp, is large and ugly and looks like a haunted house. The salt breeze has worn off whatever paint was once on it. The boys in their excitement hurried on ahead. I strolled along slowly, breathing in the fresh salt air, looking at a sand bank way out in the water, far beyond the breakers, where my friends and I fished a long time ago for bass and bluefish, thinking how easy it was for me to take my first active part in the integration movement. When I arrived at the large building, I could see from the outside that several white families were inside, evidently settling their own boys in for the camp session. I went inside.

There is a great room on the bottom floor of this building, big enough for nineteen beds. My boys had already found the ones carefully marked for them, all scattered among the other beds. It occurred to me after a minute or two that no one was saying anything. Mothers, fathers, a sister, several little brothers, the three white campers, and a dog were all strangely quiet on this first day of camp. Being separated from each other by cots, my boys were quiet too. One family, whose son is kind of chubby and has sandy hair and looks as if he'd be lots of fun at camp, I recognized. The man is a banker in a small town in the Carolina lowcountry. His wife is very pretty and was wearing a trim, white dress that set off her summer tan. I had met them at a bankers' convention several years ago. I don't think they recognized me.

The expression on the face of the banker was the same as that on the faces of the other parents in this room, serious but somehow blank. I know all these people! They aren't from Charleston, though they have many relatives there. They themselves live in small towns in the lower part of the state where their parents lived before them. The men went to some college in South Carolina, the women may have used the money set aside for their college to go to Europe. They have lived and worked in their small towns all their lives, some of them banking, some farming, some selling, all raising families, all straining to set aside enough money so that their children will be able to go to college and have the same chances in life that they had. These are the people who make the world go round, beloved and lovely.

In South Carolina, especially in the country and in small towns, things do not change easily. We're always one of the last states to try something new. It's not only conservative politics; it's the nature of the people. A friend of mine who lives in the country is a Baptist and is quite anxious to join our church. Though our church has let him know several times that he'd be most welcome, he hasn't changed yet; and this thing has been going on for ten years. I guess when you watch, as your parents before you watched, the fields plowed, the crop planted, then harvested — year after year — you get used to a fixed pattern of life, used to things as they are.

Just a few years ago these three families, who are now watching their sons unload ten days of clothing onto beds next to Negro boys, were sent an ultimatum from Washington. You cannot continue your way of life. Those colored families who live in their shacks on the other side of town and work for you as servants are as good as you are. You can no longer be separate from them. These same three families fought that ultimatum and they fought hard. Wouldn't you? Washington was telling them that a way of life as fixed as the seasonal cycle must change, now, or pretty close to now. Sure they fought. They put their heads together and figured out all the ways they could slow up Washington. Some in their midst wanted to revive the Klan; but these people are a peace-loving people, furthermore, they love, in a way which only a Southerner can understand, those people who live in the shacks across town. How could they tolerate violence? No, no Klan, there would be no violence. Their fight took place in the courts, in shrewd political moves, in the founding of private schools. They fought hard and well, swifter than eagles, stronger than lions.

Most of their friends are still fighting, but these three families have fallen in the midst of battle. They have finally realized that the old order must give way to the new — it just has to, that's all — that unless this camp is integrated, it can no longer remain in operation, that the most important thing their parents stood for and they have stood for must go if they are to live productive lives in this century, if they are to give their children the chance their parents gave them. Several months ago they read in the diocesan magazine about the integration of the camp this summer. After long and painful thought, they agreed to send their children anyway. They knew what they were getting into, they knew the camp might be integrated substantially though surely they had their hopes that no Negroes would apply. They knew it would be hard. Now the day is here. Their boys will be sharing showers and towels and games with Negro boys from backgrounds much like those who live across town in shacks.

Would you say anything? Would your expression be anything but serious and blank? This isn't nominal integration such as you find in northern churches; this isn't enforced integration brought on by government duress. These are people who are voluntarily sending their boys to sleep next to Negroes. These are people who are dying to the old order so that their children may live. How would you face death? Would you talk about it glibly and lightly? Would you brush it aside as though it doesn't matter? Or would you do as these parents are doing? Quietly help your son unload his clothes. Help him make up his bed. Kiss him good-bye and whisper to him that he must remember to brush his teeth, say his prayers, and write. Then walk quietly away. I wanted to go over and shake their hands, but how could I? My face is the face of the enemy. They don't want my praise. The banker may have recognized me, but he does not want to know me now.

After a few more minutes, I realized that I couldn't take the silence so I gave each of my boys a pocket-size New Testament and a Boy Scout handshake and slipped away, quiet and humbled. The mighty have fallen in battle today.

Tell it not in Gath, publish it not in the streets of Ashkelon lest the daughters of the Philistines rejoice, lest the daughters of the uncircumcised exult. Weep, you glib South-haters, weep! You who exalt yourselves at cocktail parties for your liberal ideas, tearing down the backward South, weep! You who damn segregation from your high pulpits and send your children to private schools, weep! You who campaign around the nation and sit fat and happy in the suburbs of Washington, swarming over the South like a plague of locusts, weep! Weep, you bastards, take off your hats, victory is yours, better men than you have died today, WEEP! How are the mighty fallen in the midst of battle.

July 20. Now where do I go from here? I was humbled yesterday and hope to stay that way, but I can't turn back from the work I'm involved in — I must fight so that my boys will have a chance. If I have another opportunity to get some of these fellows in this camp, I'll take advantage of it.

But I tell you what I'm not going to do. I am not going to see those militant or "pushing" civil rights people as I had planned. This morning, I threw away the name and address of a seminarian a school in New York sent down to us to help us solve our race problems. Maybe his job — keeping the pressure on the South — is more important than mine, but you know, I don't want anything to do with him, at least not right now. Intellectually, I can see the importance of his job; emotionally, I am not equipped to deal with him. I think of him as an enemy much in the same way that those three families thought of me as an enemy yesterday.

About midday, a young minister came by and asked me to go out to dinner with him. Much to the horror of the women standing near us in the cafeteria line, I gave him my usual talk on how we must get willing white people involved in work of a personal nature among the Negroes, especially the Negro children. I finished what I had to say about the time he finished dessert. His response: "They won't go along. I doubt if you find any 'willing white people.'"

"Well, *how* do you know that?"

"Because what you are talking about is too close to home. They may be glad for you to do it, but they won't do it themselves."

"I used to think that too, but I saw something yesterday that made me change my mind." I told him all about the camp.

"Remember, two things, Bill" (only people from my home call me by my given name): "one, those parents at the camp were not from Charleston; two, they probably won't send their sons back next year."

"Bull! I have more faith in the folks around here than you do. No, the parents weren't from Charleston, but they aren't so very different from Charlestonians. And I'll bet the boys do go back there next year. People need to experience equal personal relationships with Negroes, that's what they need. And

that's what those kids at camp are getting. If guys like yourself will lead the way by doing volunteer work among the Negroes, instead of just sitting around making cynical remarks,
we may get somewhere."

I wasn't as angry at this young man as this statement makes
me sound. I like him. He's the kind of person to whom you
can say most anything you want. He'll listen and often end up
agreeing with you, as he did at lunch. I found out later that
this minister is one of the hardest-working in the diocese.

Tonight was the big night for the hootenanny. Linda, Sally,
and I made posters and placed them all around the neighborhood so that everyone would know to come. The Catholic
seminarian who was to do the playing rounded up three
other seminarians and five "singing nuns," all white, and also
offered to furnish us with food. Michael (Adam's assistant,
who has been fired and re-hired by Father Andrews three
times in the last six months) suggested that, since it was so
hot these days, we have the program outside and use the
graves for seats. Then we could call it "The Graveyard
Smash."

When the appointed hour arrived, no one was there — except Linda, the seminarians, the nuns, and one nine-year-old
girl. At the beginning of the summer, this apparent failure of
a program I had done my best to advertise would have been
horribly discouraging. But not now. I'm learning. I knew
what we had to do. I got Olin, one of the Catholic fellows,
and his guitar, and we walked up and down the street a couple
of times strumming and singing. Before we knew it, we had a
good-size crowd gathering around us. One thing about my
voice, it creates interest. We must have ended up with a hun-

dred and fifty kids. They enjoyed the singing, but I think they enjoyed the refreshments more. It took them a while to learn the songs. They don't seem to know many outside of the religious ones they sing at church. The Peter, Paul and Mary freedom songs were completely unfamiliar.

One they learned in a hurry, one that I really liked, aesthetically and theologically, went like this:

> Christ is black, my brothers, Christ is black,
> Christ is white, my brothers, Christ is white,
> Christ is love, my brothers, Christ is love,
> Oh Lord, Christ is love.

I think those people who say that Christ is neither black nor white are quite wrong. They make Christ colorless and themselves colorless. Christ is both — black and white.

All in all, our ecumenical sing was a success. We talked of having another one soon. The Catholics said they were going to bring their bishop next time; I think I'll ask mine to come too.

Freddie was there for the hootenanny. He talked and joked with Adam all the way through it; and after it was over, he asked me to take him home. As we drove along into the wider ghetto, Freddie pointed out places where he had worked with young people. "See dat corner. I grabbed a boy on dat corner, right on the verge of big trouble. He's a Young American Citizen now, and he's goin' good. All dat boy needed was somebody to talk a little tough to him. Somebody dat knew him, that is."

"How you know all those fellows, Freddie?"

"I spent most of my life, when I warn't sick, on dem same corners. You know, dat's what the trouble is in our city right now. There's too many street corners. Dose boys get to standin' round talking, and 'fore your know it, they's in trouble. But they don't mess round with Mr. Freddie, no suh."

It was about ten o'clock and I suddenly realized that we were driving in Jackson Street Panther territory. The Panthers are the most talked-about club in Charleston. You really don't know what to believe about them. My night world people tell many stories about the Panthers. Some say they are part of a large national organization that has its headquarters in New York. Some say they've killed four or five people. Some say they have a couple of hundred members. One person told me that the authorities got a confession of murder from three of the Panthers, sixteen-year-old boys, in the following manner. There had been a murder by *someone*, there was no doubt about that. When the three boys were arrested, they were taken immediately to Columbia, South Carolina, one hundred miles away, and — terrified — they were subjected to the toughest kind of questioning. Then, each was put in a separate room and, one by one, told by the authorities: "All right, your two friends have admitted that they were at the scene of the murder, and they both say *you* pulled the trigger." In order to defend himself, each boy said that he was at the scene but it was one of the other two who pulled the trigger — not him. On hearing about this interrogation, my friend told me, the judge threw the case out. Though my friend is very trustworthy and is in a position to know, I have no proof that this story about the Panthers is true. Things like this are kept very "hush-hush" in my home town.

But the Panthers also have their friends. Sister Margaret has done a lot of work with them and speaks of them as "my Panthers." The older members of the Boys Club look up to the Panthers and talk of joining in a couple of years. You can always spot them. They wear their hair long and slick, often leaving a comb in the hair itself. And they all dress well.

I tried not to let Freddie know that I was afraid of his neighborhood when he asked me to come in to meet his parents. As we walked toward his apartment, Freddie introduced me to a dozen or so people who came out from behind dark windows on seeing a white person pass by at night. Two of them, obviously Panthers, shook my hand in a friendly manner and responded with a grin to Freddie's chiding them about their long hair, a thing few people in town could get away with. After meeting several of Freddie's neighbors, I realized that I was completely safe. Everyone likes Freddie. "Since you're his friend," said one tough-looking guy, "that's good enough for me." Freddie's parents didn't know whether to get up or stay seated when I walked into the room; but after that brief moment of embarrassment, we were relaxed with each other. On the way out, Freddie showed me those model planes that really fly. On the floor of his closet — three dirty planes, fingered by perhaps fifty different slum children, put together crudely, each with a string attached to one of the wings, a string which could be used to make the planes twirl around and around overhead. "We fly 'em high," Freddie said as we parted.

What would I do without you Mr. Freddie?

July 21: Today, Edward Black-y-mo Gray cried for the first time. When his friends tease him about his especially dark skin, his ragged clothes, or his bad speech, he fights them, three or four at a time; but he never cries. When the older boys, like Zookie, push him around and kick him like a dog while he grovels in the dirt, he smiles, proud that he can take all their punishment. When he goes without meals, sometimes for a day at a time, he plays and laughs just as hard as ever. Edward is a happy boy and a brave boy and doesn't believe in tears.

But today was the day that Linda and I took the little boys and girls on their outing — without Edward. I had been talking this trip up for a long time, about how we'd drive in a *car* — "no bus for us, no bus for us" — some twenty miles, even crossing the Cooper River Bridge, how we'd take a walk in the woods and collect pine cones and crab and do all those things. I made a point of getting Edward excited about the trip. He and Richard are the most neglected of the kids at the center, and I like to see them have fun. Like Richard, Black-y-mo is easy to get attached to. During one of my sermonettes, I got him to play the part of the paralytic who was lowered through the roof for Jesus to heal. Of course, we couldn't tear out the ceiling, but we did manage to lower Edward on something of a pallet from two tall stepladders outside the chapel doorway. Goodie, who played Jesus, then healed him. Frozen in a contorted position revealing the extent of the paralysis, Edward, when he felt Goodie's touch, smiled — in fact he laughed — stood up, examined his new limbs, and walked proudly into the chapel, swinging his arms and legs as far as they would swing. Everyone cheered this remarkable feat. Next to me, Edward enjoys my sermonettes more than anyone.

There was a rumor circulating today that Edward was not to go on the outing. Since he denied all this talk, I thought I'd better check with his mother. All summer I have avoided making this call, afraid of what I would see. Even at the bottom of society, there's a bottom. Linda tells me that one of Edward's six sisters died last spring, mainly from starvation, and that the mother has been out of work for some time. I suspected that I would find that bottom today. I did. Edward agreed to lead me to his home. People just could not live in worse conditions.

We went down the street from the center around the corner and stopped in front of one of those big three-story buildings, unpainted, uncared for, that house an unknown number of people. "Do you live here Edward?" I asked.

"Ah lib afor nit."

"What?"

"Ah lib afor nit."

Edward is said to have a terrible speech impediment, but I wonder if he's ever been taught how to talk. Usually, I try to make out what he's saying by myself, but today, I had to ask one of the boys playing with rocks on the sidewalk what Edward was trying to tell me.

"He says he lives in the backyard," the little boy answered.

We walked on back. There was a one-room wooden shack back there, with no window frames, no door in the entrance way. It was built on supports several feet off the ground. Children were sitting on the steps. It looked like a stable, only worse. More children were leaning out of the window opening. God, how do people live like this? Babies were lying on the floor inside, crying. I can't go in. The smell was of urine and burning newspaper. I can't take this.

So I talked to a girl, who looked about ten, on the steps. Edward's mother was not in, but this little girl, in charge, said most emphatically that her brother was not to go on the outing today. Something about his having to go to the hospital on account of his sores, which I noticed were much worse.

I put my hand on Edward's shoulder. "That's okay, big fellow, we'll get you on another trip soon, really, we will."

Edward didn't say a word, didn't make a noise. He grabbed his little green shirt with both hands at the place where the top button should be and pulled it up over his face and wept, and wept. It seemed as if all the misery of that young, broken life flowed to the surface in those tears. And Jesus wept.

O Christ! I can't stand this. "Edward, don't cry, boy, there'll be another chance." But once started, Edward could not stop.

What do you do? Tell me, what do you do? Don't give me any of your pat answers. Tell me, what do I do right now? What can I do?

I'll tell you what I did. I did what we Americans usually do when we become frustrated and see no way out. If we can't do the job, the DOLLAR will. I tried to buy my way out. "Come here, young fellow" — I motioned to the boy who had done the interpreting for me — "take this quarter down to the store and buy Edward and yourself a soda."

I gave him the money and got out of that backyard as fast as I could, even faster than I got out of that room at camp. Edward was leaning against the wall now, his head still buried in his shirt. As I walked away, putting my wallet back in my pocket, I thought about the hand-me-down people on the other side of town and about our hand-me-down government. We aren't so different.

July 22:   No entry.

July 23:   No entry.

July 24:   No entry.

July 25:   No entry.

July 26: Thinking nothing. Lying on my bed in the junk room. Shapes on the ceiling. Nothing. Watermarks? Shadows? Goddam sunlight coming through the window. Playing tricks on me. Lying in my sweat on the bed. Not hot. Not chilled. I see a great big bird, Mama. Not tired. Not frustrated. Nothing. See, he's all there except for a wing. And look at that crooked river. It's a funny old river, isn't it? *The little toy soldier is red with rust, and the musket moulds in his hand. . . . Now don't you go till I come, he said. . . . The years are many and the years are long since he kissed them and put them there.** Why did the little boy have to die, Mama? And don't you make any noise. Pull down the shade. Why? That's a sad story, Mama, don't tell it to me again. I don't want to know about death. I see a tiger now, see. Don't go away. Please Mother, please don't leave me. . . . Please dear God, please. Why did it have to happen? I've been doing a good job, haven't I, haven't I? Working my butt off, suffering with those people at camp. Father Andrews told me so. All these last few days and then all at once this morning. Goddam light! Lying in bed. O Lord, may I never see a poem as lovely as a tree. Rivers, tigers, clouds, deserts, sunlight. Freddie dead? Who told you, young fellow? Hey, is there anything to the rumor that that fellow who was going to be the scoutmaster is dead? I saw him yesterday. My hope, Freddie you can't die. Fool, dead fool. Yes, my son had been sick all his life and finally this morning about four o'clock the

* The lines in italics are quoted from Eugene Field's poem, "Little Boy Blue."

Lord saw fit to carry Freddie away. Das right. Das right. They gave him some oxygen, but it was too late. But staunch and sturdy he stands. Mother! My boy has gone and only twenty-six. Ha! That's very funny, I've been telling everyone he's much older than I am. That's funny, Mama. Tell me another one. And how come you're so calm, Mrs. Johnson? I always thought Negroes raised hell and carried on like crazy at times like these. Yes, I nursed Freddie most of my life. He was a good boy — but never made it past the seventh grade. Freddie had the will — but he had no way. Yes, Father Andrews that was — sort of a prophetic statement. Why don't you scream? Do you know something about death that I don't? We took him down to the hospital and they gave him some oxygen — but Freddie's heart had just given out. Tears. Sunlight. Poor boy spent half his life in bed. Mother. Model airplanes. Why did Little Boy Blue have to. . . . And as he was dreaming, an angel song. . . . Your son was a good man, one of the best I've met. I shall always remember him. God bless you, Mr. Freddie. All the living he had. Heart had given out.

Who are you, little girl? O sure I remember now. You are Edward Gray's big sister, the one who wouldn't let him go on the trip. No, I don't think I can come over to see your mother this morning. Don't cry, little girl. Oh goddammit, little girl, don't cry. Sure, I'll come over. Squalor. Stink. Urine. Niggers. The years are many and the years are long since he kissed them and put them. . . . Sickness. What do you *do?* Lying in the bed. Deserts, clouds, tigers, watermarks. Come on, Mama, tell me. What happened to that broken wing. I'll bet you know. You're teasing me. Why can't I leave some fruitcake on Great-grandfather's grave? Why won't he get it when we leave? Sweat. Blessed sweat. Darkness. Blessed darkness. Now I lays me down to sleep. Prays the Lord my soul to keep. Nothing. MY GOD WOMAN YOU MEAN YOU HAVEN'T FED YOUR CHILDREN A THING IN THREE DAYS. No wonder some of them are so sick they can't move. What do you expect? I'm sorry, I didn't mean to raise my voice. Don't cry. Don't make me go back and fight him. He can beat me up. Yes, I can see for myself. Only salt and pepper. A little bit of salt and a little bit of pepper. God in heaven! The Welfare Department? The Salvation Army? The Church? No relatives at all? Nothing? Nothing? What are you going to do? Stay away, light. Pull down the shade, Mother. Deserts. Rocking a baby in her arms. Squirming in bed. When the bough breaks, the cradle will. . . . You say you had income until a few weeks ago and. . . . No, don't tell me how you made it. I've heard. You're a pretty woman, but you shouldn't make money like that. And you probably did it right in front of your children too. Dirty . . . crawling . . . niggers. I know you did it to buy food, but that's goddam awful. I don't know why I backed down, Daddy. What makes your baby shake so much? Tell them all to quit crying. I'll leave. Yes, I will. It doesn't bother you that I might leave? How are you so calm? You mean you owe two months' rent? We've got little money ourselves. Where will it come from? Thinking nothing. Mrs. Gray, you mean you'd do even *that* for your children. I know what Jesus said. Greater love has no man than this that he would lay down his life for his friends. But. . . . And you like Mrs. Johnson are calm. You've done your best and you are now waiting for the Lord to take you or to save you. There's no more fight left, is there? Is death really no mystery, no great thing to be feared? A time for livin' and a time for dyin'. Do your best and let God do the rest. You're a beautiful woman, Mrs. Gray. I'll be back. Somehow I'll be back with help. Keep up the good spirits. Sunlight. Day worlds. Freddie. Life.

And I stayed and I listened to Mrs. Gray. And I wept, not out loud, but I wept. And this time I did not run; but I stayed and I watched with Mrs. Gray. Death, where is thy sting? Blessed daylight. Thank you, my God in heaven. Thank you. I'm all right now. I'm up and won't go back to bed. I shall keep my promise and go back with help this afternoon. And I will find someone to take Freddie's place. And tonight, we will have the big dance Freddie helped us advertise.

VI

And a Time for Living

I was by myself now, away from whites and blacks, welfare workers and Mary Belle Grays. It was not the "nigger-hating" country boys who live in Hell-Hole Swamp that I was afraid of. . . . But out there in the silence of the woods, in the darkness of the night, I was afraid. . . . Am I letting myself become too involved in this difficult question of race relations? What is the ultimate meaning of all this, anyway? If I am fighting against the world that raised me, whom can I run to for comfort now? Alone in the stillness of the night.

◑

*Do you not know that all of
us who have been baptized into
Christ Jesus were baptized into
his death? We were buried therefore with him by baptism into
death, so that as Christ was
raised from the dead by the glory
of the Father, we too might walk
in newness of life.*

— Romans

JULY 27.

```
Hi Batmen                    Hi Robbins
         COME SOME    COME ALL
                  to the
           BIG DANCE

   Eight o'clock till The Pot o' Honey
        Sponsored by the Saxons
   PLAYED BY ART THE MUSIC MAN
   At 18 Blank Street          Ad. 50¢
```

When Goodie is not playing Jesus in my sermonettes, he often does artwork, such as this poster and the nine others like it which he made up to advertise the dance last night. The Boys Club, which is sponsoring the dance, placed these posters around their section of town — in Mr. Dick's grocery store, in a barber shop, in a shoeshine shop, in a couple of hamburger places. The rest they hung up in the center itself.

The Saxons are a defunct club consisting of Adam, Michael, and a few other fellows from this neighborhood. It is the successor to a gang of hoodlums that almost went the way of the Jackson Street Panthers and probably would have if it hadn't been for Father Andrews who worked with these young hoods and steered them toward responsible club activity and away from criminality. Though the club is defunct, the Saxons' name is widely known; and, like the name of Art the Music Man, it makes any poster better. During a rump meeting of Adam, Michael, and a few others, it was decided that the Boys Club could use their name on the posters.

Art works by day on some anti-poverty program and by night as a disc jockey and at dances like ours last night. You really get your money's worth with Art. He brought two drummers, four dancers, and six prizes along with him. He himself spun records, danced and sang along, dubbing in lines with local color. Art and his group were on time. As usual, none of the young people, except the Boys Club had come. But Art didn't let that bother him. He took the mike and addressed the large empty room as though it were packed with people: "Ladies and Gentlemen, tonight we are going to dance to all your favorite tunes; there'll be fast ones and slow ones, old ones and new ones, jumpin' ones and blue ones; dance one, dance all, big prizes await the coolest cat and his mate. Are you ready, Drummer John? Yes, you are. Are you ready, little disc? Yes you are. Roll around, little disc, play, Drummer John, play, little disc, dance one, dance all to the Co-o-o-o-o-o-o-o-ol JERK." Of course, no one was dancing, except for Art that is. He sang and twisted around up there on the little stage at the end of the nave as much at the beginning of the dance, when the place was empty, as he did later on, when it was packed.

Shortly after Art got the dance started, Police Officer Jones,

a heavy-set, middle-aged Negro, arrived to keep the party orderly. Last night was his night off, but he agreed to come anyway — and without pay. He has the reputation for being the
toughest man alive. Not even the Panthers mess with him.
Officer Jones, widely known as the Candy Man behind his
back, lived up to his reputation last night.

We put Michael, our biggest and strongest staff member, at
the door, Linda got one of the Negro teachers to join him
there, aware that a female would have a stabilizing influence
at the place where the trouble would be most apt to start, the
place where lots of people would try to break through without
paying. The Boys Club manned their positions behind the soft
drinks table. Sneed had given them instructions as to what
they should do if someone did not pay. "If he's smilin', make
him pay de dime; if he's mean, give 'em de Coke."

About nine o'clock the guests began arriving. Most were
between the ages of sixteen and twenty-one. Not many came
in couples but most were in groups of threes and fours. There
must have been a hundred and fifty there altogether. I found
out during the dance that they came from the West Side as
well as the East Side. There were a few Jackson Street Panthers there, several large, unattractive girls, who would have
been wallflowers at any other dance, a lot of guys dressed to
look tough, many good-looking girls, a few fellows with horn-
rimmed glasses, who looked as though they might be students
somewhere. There were coats and ties, shorts and sandals,
long dresses and short dresses. I noticed one cat who fell into
a class all of his own. In addition to very dark glasses and a
black suit and black tie, he wore a red shirt and carried an
umbrella under his arm all night.

The young people didn't seem to want to dance at first; but

with the prodding from Art's troop, they finally began swinging. I mean I saw some dances. The Cool Jerk, the Pot
o' Honey, and Good Night were the most popular. Soon everyone was dancing, the large, unattractive girls, the tough guys.
Everyone. If you didn't have a partner, you just got out on
the floor and got the feeling that made you want to dance and
shout. "DANCE MAN, DANCE," Art kept screaming into
the mike. Young lovers found each other and didn't hesi-
tate to show their mutual affection at the Big Dance. Everyone had the rhythm, the swing, except of course for Linda,
Officer Jones, and myself, the only real wallflowers there.

About halfway through the dance, a West Side cat hit one
of the East-Siders over the head. Almost instantaneously, two
gangs emerged from among the crowd of dancers and would
certainly have started a melee if it had not been for the
Candy Man. He merely pulled out his billy stick, swung it
back and forth by the leather strap, and walked over to where
the trouble was. The crowd divided to make a path for him.
Officer Jones then proceeded to throw out anyone who looked
at all guilty. Shoving these potential troublemakers out of the
door, into the graveyard outside, he saw someone sitting on his
patrol car. "Get off," he bellowed at the young man, about
nineteen or twenty. But the guy didn't move. Officer Jones
pulled out his thirty-eight and pointed it at this fellow's fore-
head. "Now, get off." The boy got off. There was no trouble
during the rest of the evening.

It was probably Art who kept us from getting into trouble
with the city. Right before the Pot o' Honey, the last dance,
he got everyone there to repeat after him several times: "We
are young ladies and gentlemen, and we will not — repeat, not
— set off the fire alarm outside the center tonight." I was

sure that vow would be an invitation to do the opposite; but Art knew best. The glass was unbroken this morning.

We did rather well collecting money from the people who came to the dance. Only about one-fourth got through without paying; and we lost only $5 on the soft drinks. After we paid Art and his troop their fee of $35, which included the $10 Art spent on the prizes, we still had $8 in the shoe box — clear profit for the Boys Club. Already they have decided on several hundred dollars' worth of equipment which they will purchase with their profit. Policeman Jones wouldn't talk to me or to anyone else during the dance. But after it was all over, and we were drinking Cokes and thinking about how we would clean up the mess on the dance floor, I was surprised to find this tough cop just as nice a fellow as you'd meet anywhere. He even laughed at himself and his reputation around town when some of the younger boys teased him.

During most of the dance, I had sat on the sidelines, unmistakably white. Things are changing for me, I thought to myself. Up until now, I have been so anxious to *do* something worthwhile for the Negroes of Charleston. When I went to see Freddie's parents and then stayed and wept with Mrs. Gray, going back to take her money for rent and food for her children this afternoon, I probably came as close to doing something worthwhile for the Negro as I ever will. But something's different, I thought as I sat there. It's not so much what I've done that is giving me satisfaction, it's what's being done for me. Here I am, not really an invited guest either of the Big Dance or of the ghetto but, nevertheless, a guest who is tolerated and treated kindly. And right now, at this precise moment of time, I feel fulfilled, at one with myself, at one with God. I am being allowed to share in great things, events as great as Jacob's wrestling with God. Instead of doing something for these people, they're doing something for me. They are showing me — these mothers in distress, these cool cats and their suggestive dances — how life even in the midst of the death, the squalor, the injustice, the toughness of the ghetto, how life can not only be endured, but — loved. God and man meet; both triumphant. DANCE, MAN, DANCE. Live, man, live. Freddie would have enjoyed the Big Dance.

When I got home, it was already late; but I kept my wife up for two more hours telling her all about the events of the day. I made up a prayer while I was drifting off to sleep. It went something like this: "As Goodie asked his people to come some, come all to his Big Dance, let us, O Lord, come one, come all to your Big Dance. Thank you, Lord, for letting me be with you, both during the morning and the evening watch."

July 28. Up until today, I had been under the illusion that our society would not let children in its midst starve to death. That was before I went with Mrs. Gray to the Charleston County Welfare Department in the old Citadel Building, just a few blocks from the center. This is what happened:

To begin with, I had a struggle getting Mrs. Gray to leave her children. Yesterday, in fact, she would not go with me. Armed with the charisma bestowed upon me by the Big Dance, I had gone to see her bright and early in hopes that she and I together could find aid for her family. She said, however, she could not leave her children as long as they were so sick. And besides, the Welfare Department hadn't helped her at all when she lost her last child. Today, I was more firm. "Look, Mrs. Gray," I said, "the Welfare Department has a rule, which they will not break, that they will not come to an individual's home until the case has been opened by the individual's first coming for an interview with them. That rule may sound unfair to you when you are nursing sick children but the law is the law. Our aim is to get aid for those children, one way or another, and the Welfare Department is the logical place to start." Since the children were better today, having eaten regularly for the last two days, she finally agreed to go with me. The nine-year-old girl and Black-y-mo were left in charge.

We were met at the door of the Welfare Department by a receptionist who listened closely as I told of Mrs. Gray's great need, of how her children were on the verge of starvation, of how she hadn't fed them from Friday until Tuesday, of how we were a small mission with a small budget, and of how one of her children had already starved to death. "We need help," I pleaded, "right now, before other members of her family, other members of society die." This lady, who has a pleasant face and an understanding nature, sympathized with the situation but said the best she could do for us was to make an appointment a week from tomorrow. "Her children may not be living a week from tomorrow, don't you see. This situation is urgent." I knew very well that I'd keep Mrs. Gray in food if I had to do so out of my own pocket, but I wanted to make a point.

"Very well," said the receptionist, "let me talk with my supervisor." She left for about fifteen minutes; and when she returned, she said that perhaps one of the case workers could see me, if I didn't mind waiting a while. Two hours later, the case worker called me in. Like the receptionist, she was very nice and sympathetic. She even knew several of my relatives. But this young lady, who seems to be doing the job she is charged with, came close to destroying my faith, not only in our government but in the people of our land as well.

She began by giving me a summary of the Welfare Department's record of Mrs. Gray and her family. It seems that for the six children, there are four fathers, the father of Edward and the next oldest girl being the legal husband. When Mrs. Gray came to the Welfare Department the last time, she was told that before the case could be considered and a worker call on her home, she must present adequate proof that she had received no aid from any of the fathers. First, she would have to obtain letters from the last-known employers and landlords certifying that they did not know of the men's whereabouts. Second, she would have to get statements from three neighbors that none of the men had been seen at the Gray's home. Third, if Mrs. Gray was able to locate the legal husband, she would have to make an attempt through the Domestic Court to get support from him. If she was able to locate any of the others, she would have to report to the Magistrate's Court. After she had collected all these statements and notified the courts in the proper way, she could then return to the Welfare Department, which had ninety days in which to consider her request. Mrs. Gray did not come for her next appointment with the case worker.

I tried to discuss the matter reasonably with the young lady in front of me. I did not want to cut her off by losing my temper and my perspective as I had done at the hospital, but I did argue that this whole welfare system is grossly unfair. I described the gravity of Mrs. Gray's situation, going into the details of filth and poverty. Then I said that those required statements and court visits were hard enough for me to understand and that surely they must be completely above the comprehension of Mrs. Gray, who dropped out of school at age thirteen to have her first baby. "And besides, even if she wanted to, she could not leave her children to go searching all over town for those four men, three of whom she hasn't seen in over two years."

But this case worker assured me that she could do nothing until Mrs. Gray obtained those statements and tried to get help from the courts. Furthermore, she said that there was no local, state, or federal means of public support until the case is settled, that there was no public means of helping Mrs. Gray establish proof of her nonsupport — she did not know of any private organization that did this sort of work either — and finally that there was no appeal until the case had been turned down, presumably months from now. "What about those kids that may die, your department will not consider them?" I was beginning to let go. "I can give you all the proof you want of a desperate need in this situation, more proof than all that other stuff combined, if only you will go with me to call on this family, go with me and see babies lying in the filth on the floor, see a kitchen that was empty of everything except salt and pepper until I, by chance, happened to visit there."

"I'm sorry," she answered, "but we do not have the funds to call on people until some kind of *legal* proof of need is established, unless of course the individual is mentally or physically unable to gather the necessary documents." She sounded like my military instructors, reciting law such-and-such, code such-and-such, of act SUCH-AND-SUCH. "Now if you will let me see Mrs. Gray by herself," she continued, "then I'll speak again with you." I went outside and waited some more, trying to control myself. There had been a time, I was thinking to

myself, when I thought the impossibleness of government bu-
reaucracy a laughing matter.

Mrs. Gray came out. I went in. The case worker told me
substantially the same things all over again. I didn't even argue this time. When I was leaving, she said to me, "Inciden-
tally, we need all those statements by next Thursday or the
case will have to be closed again."

"Next Thursday, one week? If Mrs. Gray and I do this job
right, it'll take all our working hours for the next two weeks."

"I'm sorry, but rules are rules."

Yes indeed, rules are rules. But something is dreadfully
wrong with this welfare system — not with the case worker,
hers is a grueling, thankless, no doubt greatly underpaid job —
but something is sick in the system. If the Welfare
Department was dealing with people from an average low-
class background, this system conceivably might be acceptable.
But the indigent persons who really need welfare come from
the bottom of society. They are the Mary Belle Gray's,
women with four husbands for six children, women so beaten
down by society that they wouldn't dare go to a "previous employer" and ask for a legal statement, women practically illit-
erate. What do they know about "establishing reasonable
proof," about going to the Domestic Court? All that talk is
nothing more than babble to a person like Black-y-mo's
mother. It's not much more than that to me. Mrs. Gray didn't
want to return to the Welfare Department. Would you?

Our government has failed in its responsibility to meet the
needs of its starving citizens. Somewhere, maybe right this
minute, right in this city, a kid is dying of starvation because
of the ineptitude of our government. But let's be careful
about indicting the government; that shifts the blame to some

vague entity the internal workings of which no one under-
stands anyway. What I want to know is: why has no church
or civic organization, worthy of those titles, found out what
goes on at the Welfare Department and made some attempt
to help people like Mrs. Gray fight through the red tape?
Why has no one, Negro or white, done anything to help Mrs.
Gray until now? Why for God's sake haven't we American
citizens as individuals found out what goes on in the ghetto —
instead of leaving it all up to the Salvation Army and the
Welfare Department.

I've lived in Charleston most of my life. How come I've
never thought about the fact that people die of starvation in
this beautiful and historic city by the sea? Why is it that no
one told me? Why is it that I didn't find out for myself? I
remember one servant that my mother hired "off the street"
who was so hungry that she ate most everything in the icebox
before she was able to work. Why didn't I think to ask this
woman what her children at home had eaten during the last
two weeks? Like most everyone else, I guess I thought that
since this is twentieth-century America, we are too *advanced*
to let people in our midst starve.

Our society will never be great as long as its individual citizens are so irresponsible. Sorry, Mr. President, it can't work.
Ironically enough, the Southern politicians are quite right
when they say that the government is not bigger than the people in it. It certainly isn't bigger than many of them.

After the mighty King David had committed adultery with
Bathsheba and sent Uriah her husband to die in battle, he was
told this story by the prophet Nathan:

> There were two men in a certain city, the one rich and the
> other poor. The rich man had very many flocks and herds;

but the poor man had nothing but one little ewe lamb, which he had bought. And he had brought it up, and it grew up with him and with his children; it used to eat of his morsel, and drink from his cup, and lie in his bosom, and it was like a daughter to him. Now there came a traveler to the rich man, and he was unwilling to take one of his own flock or herd to prepare for the wayfarer who had come to him, but he took the poor man's lamb, and prepared it for the man who had come to him.

David was sad for the poor man and his anger was greatly kindled against the rich man. He said to the prophet Nathan, "As the Lord lives, the man who has done this deserves to die; and he shall restore the lamb fourfold, because he did this thing, and because he had no pity."

Nathan pointed his finger at David and said to him, "You are the man." Some kid is starving right now. Who's really responsible? Who's really the guilty one? The case worker? The government? No! No. YOU are the man! *I* am the man.

July 29. Since Father Andrews will be leaving on his vacation this Monday, he called me into his office today in order to give me a small discretionary fund and some last minute instructions. It's funny, but with my interest in Mrs. Gray's case and in the other events of the past few days, I'm not at all worried about taking over Father Andrews's position for this next month, as I thought I would be. While we talked, it was obvious to both of us that our conversation was stiff and formal. Why is it that I cannot relax with this man? Is it because I find him too disorganized for my bank and Coast Guard disciplined self? Is it because I'm prejudiced? Why is it that he cannot relax with me? I think each of us appreciates the other, but only on a few occasions this summer have either of us been able to express this appreciation.

He is going up to New England for three or four weeks and told me not to call him unless the center burned down. After working in the ghetto less than two months, I'm already becoming emotionally and physically tired. He's been at it for four or five years. I don't think I'll interrupt his vacation even if the center does burn down.

July 30. In contrast to what happened at the Welfare Department, the events this morning helped to reaffirm my faith in people — at least in children not yet corrupted by society.

This morning, I drove down to the camp where I left the five boys ten days ago. When I arrived, all the campers were eating breakfast. My boys were sitting at the far table, gobbling up the corn flakes like everyone else. They waved to me when I entered; but, busy with their last morning at camp, they didn't seem too interested in seeing me. I sat at a table with three white campers and several staff members and accepted their invitation to eat a second breakfast. The boys were talking about those plastic lanyards that camps are famous for, about swimming, and about trips on which they caught buckets of crabs.

After breakfast, one of the young campers called me down for putting my tray and silverware in the wrong place. You'd think after all these years I'd be able to figure something like that out. I then sought out the nurse and talked with her for about half an hour. If she and I aren't related, it's a miracle. We must have *forty* cousins in common. But I was happy to talk family with this rather elderly lady — she had done us a big favor. Four or five days before, she had called St. Paul's Mission Center and demanded that either we get the five boys' parents to write or that we get some of the boys' friends to write. Apparently, my boys had shown up every day for the mail call, but not one had received a letter. So they just watched while the white boys received stacks of mail from their relatives. In response to this phone call, knowing that most of the parents could not write, I got Sneed and several others to write the letters. "William," the nurse said, "is still carrying a letter around in his shirt pocket from a boy named Goodie."

My prediction that all the young campers, black and white, would have fun proved to be substantially accurate. The minister in charge and I talked for a few minutes on the porch of the dining hall about how the session had gone. Two days after camp had started, there had been a fight. It seems that one of our fellows stepped on the bed of one of the white boys who promptly called him a "black nigger." Then our fellow hit him in the jaw. But after that, there was a camp meeting and open discussion about race and feelings of prejudice. The two boys who got into the fight once again became friends.

When I drove up to the haunted house to pick up the boys, I found them all packed and ready to go. Lanyards were wrapped around their necks. Sandy seashells and brightly painted plaster of Paris animals and Jesuses filled their arms. Jerome was proudly displaying his Beginner's Swimming Permit by holding it in his teeth. Their luggage — the best suitcases that could be borrowed in their section of town — lay at their feet. They were in a grand humor. The conversation returning home went something like this.

DRIVER. Well, boys, how'd it go?

DOUG. I'm going to save up so's I can go back next summer.

WILLIAM. Me too.

CHAMP. We all passed the swimming test, Mr. Barnwell. The man said we were quick learners.

DRIVER. *You* fellows? Oh, I don't believe that.

ALL. Das right, man! Das right.

WILLIAM. Doug got so good he could swim fifty feet.

DRIVER. I'd have to *see* that to believe it. By the way, how'd you get on with those white boys?

JEROME. Allen cooned one of dem white boys in he jaw. (Laughs.)

ALLEN. I'll coon you if you don't shut your mout', boy. (More laughs.)

DRIVER. I sort of had the idea you got on pretty well with them.

WILLIAM. My second best friend was a white boy.

CHAMP. Gre-a-a-a-a-a-at. . . . Listen to that boy story.

JEROME. We half-sheeted dem boys at night.

DOUG. Those fellows just dozin' you, Mr. Barnwell. We got along fine with the white boys, after the first few days anyway.

DRIVER. Well, if you had fun and they had fun, I guess you must have gotten on all right.

DOUG. Yes, suh.

WILLIAM. How 'bout stopping to get us a soda?

DRIVER. I thought you had spent all your money.

WILLIAM. Please for a dime, Mr. Barnwell.

DRIVER. Please for a dime, nuttin', William. I'm going to coon *you* in a minute. (More laughs.)

And so forth.

How easy these boys make the solution to the racial conflict sound. Even the fight was a good thing. Older and more mature people would not have called each other names and would not have hit each other, but these boys got whatever racial prejudice was eating at them off their minds right away and then were able to enjoy camp as much as ever.

And he took a child and put him in the midst of them and taking him in his arms, he said to them, "Whoever receives one such child in my name receives me; and whoever receives me, receives not me but him who sent me."

July 31. Sunday afternoon. I have just come home from Freddie's funeral. The service was held in a brightly colored chapel in a local Negro funeral home. The place was packed; I was the only white there. Freddie was lying peacefully in his coffin in the front of the chapel, not bothered by the fly crawling on his nose. In front of him was the raised stand for the undertaker and preacher. And in the center of the wall behind them, a large picture of Jesus, white; on the right, a smaller picture of the Lord's Supper; and on the left, a sign that read:

> If we please you
> tell others.
> If we don't
> tell us.

Freddie would have been pleased with his funeral. The coffin and the front of the chapel were covered with as many flowers as the Johnsons' savings would buy. All sorts of people were there to pay their last respects to Freddie. A Jackson Street Panther was a pallbearer. Most of the young people were, no doubt, members of the Young American Citizens.

There were five eulogies, the best of which, I thought, came from a young man who spoke bad English but who told about how Freddie "have work the street corners" and how "he have made leaders of young boys to follow in his pathway."

Then there was singing: "Nearer My God to Thee," "Asleep with Jesus," and "Yes, We Shall Gather at the River." And there was the usual emotion Negro funerals are known for. Things were fairly quiet until the middle of the second hymn when a voice interrupted the singing with a loud scream. "OH FREDDIE, Freddie, OH JESUS, OH Lord Jesus, Freddie, Freddie, OH GOD." Then the others started. As their emotions came so easily to the surface, I realized that tears were filling my eyes too. Mr. Freddie is dead. At one point, the screaming and singing was so loud that it seemed close to mass hysteria. Maybe this kind of release of tension helps explain why Mrs. Johnson could face her son's death with an over-all calmness and with a wisdom as ancient as the earth.

There was one other thing that would have pleased Freddie. On each seat was a cardboard fan. The name and address of the funeral home was printed on one side of the fan. On the other, there was a color picture of a Negro Boy Scout and a Negro Girl Scout standing in front of a large American flag which waved in the breeze. Underneath the picture was written: "One Nation Indivisible." I kept one of the fans.

August 1. Life is just plain strange at times, strangely beautiful. Yesterday, we buried Freddie; today, we were sent two young Negro airmen who are going to try to take his place. Furthermore, last night and this morning several little things happened which made me wonder if there might be a changing response to the racial situation among those of my white world. In my involvement with the Negro, I tend to lose sight of what's going on in the white world.

Last night, a friend — the one who wouldn't let me take one carload of boys to his country place — and I had a long conversation. Finally working up the courage to confront him and telling him how mad and disappointed I was at his refusal, I found that he wanted to talk about it too. He couldn't tell me why he refused. "It's something I don't fully understand," he said. He did tell me later in the conversation that he too had sent his children to a camp that was at least nominally integrated and that he supported the admission of a Negro boy to the private school which his son attends. "I am trying," he seemed to say. My friend could have been one of those parents at the camp I took my boys to.

This morning, after Father Andrews had come in to say good-bye I moved into his air-conditioned office and got right to work on the telephone trying to locate Mrs. Gray's missing husbands. And I heard a white man, one of the "previous employers," a man I had never met, say on the other end of the phone, "I think it's just fine that you're trying to help this woman. I wish we Methodists would follow the example of your church and become involved in race relations and in trying to improve the slum conditions." I told this man that we really weren't doing that much; but he said we were doing something, and that that was better than nothing. "Mr. Barnwell," he continued, "we tend to think that if we leave the race problem alone, it'll go away, but you know from your work and I know from mine that it'll just get worse — much, much worse."

That might not *sound* like much of a change of attitude;

but it is! An awareness of the true gravity of the situation, a new unwillingness to evade it with easy talk about how much we've always done for our Nigras, a resolve to do something about the poverty — all these taken together make an encouraging change indeed. As encouraging as an alcoholic's going to his first AA meeting.

Later in the morning at a filling station, pretending to look up directions on a city map, I listened to the manager argue with a young man about race.

"I think you're getting to be a nigger-lover," said the young man.

"Now look-a-yhere, Sonnie. Half my customers are colored. If I'm not good to them, it'll hurt my business. You ought to be able to understand that."

Rather than be run out of business by way of the back alley of dark racial hate, this filling-station manager is choosing to live productively in twentieth-century America. This conversation would not have been possible in Charleston a few years ago. It reflects not only the white man's new willingness to respond but also the Negro's nascent determination to stand up and demand proper treatment in this city.

For all his civic activity, Freddie was not the type of Negro to make that kind of stand. The two young airmen who appeared at the center late this afternoon are! Josh and Paul are from New York and Wisconsin respectively. Unlike most Southern Negroes, they immediately impress you with their self-confidence, their poise, their perfect English. Linda's ex-roommate, whom they'd met the night before at a party, suggested that they come give us a hand at St. Paul's. Josh and Paul told me that they had a lot of time off they could use more profitably than just getting drunk; and they said that they would like to work at the center doing whatever they could.

Sneed was attempting to drill the Boys Club when the two airmen arrived. Without the charismatic leadership of Mr. Freddie, the boys were almost out of control. Then Josh took over. He drilled those little boys for one hour and a half; and I believe he did more with them, as far as giving them the discipline they need, than I have done all summer. I couldn't believe my eyes. Even some of the older boys, like Zookie, who spend most of their waking hours on the street corners, joined in and seemed proud to be part of a platoon that was catching on so fast.

Only one thing spoiled the magnificent picture of Josh standing erect in front of the boys, who were responding to his every command. It was Adam. Adam, about Josh's age, dressed in clothes from the hand-me-down room, was sitting on the card table, his head bent, his feet dangling, fiddling with his beard, watching young boys from his neighborhood come alive, thinking — no telling what.

After the drill was over, I asked Josh and the other man, Paul, to come into the office to talk business. Paul was quiet, but Josh was very outgoing. He's one of those unusual Negroes you meet from time to time who possesses the best characteristics of both races. He has the openness, the friendliness, the knowledge of what really counts in life of the Negro; he has the initiative, the know-how, the self-respect of the white man. He is at once proud to be Negro and glad to have friends, such as the girl who sent him to the mission center, who are white. His father is a major in the Army; his mother organized a major Harlem political campaign. Josh has had the chances in life that I want my boys to have some day.

Unlike many such Negroes, he has not forgotten the rest of his people who have been left behind. The center will not be the first ghetto he's worked in. Before he joined the Air Force, he spent a considerable amount of time working with the poor in Harlem.

Paul and Josh agreed to take charge of the Boys Club which they want to convert into a Boy Scout troop. They agreed with me that it is better to start out with one activity and branch out after that one is well established; but already, they were talking about organizing Cub Scouts, Girl Scouts, a remedial reading program, voter registration campaigns, all the things we need so much. I told Linda after they left that something's got to be wrong. It all sounds too good to be true.

If these two young men are faithful to their plans and others from the North join them in this kind of work in the ghetto, my concept of *transitional* paternalism may not be necessary. They will do better the same things I suggested my night world people do. As my mother pointed out to me at supper, "Josh and Paul did so well because they give the young Nigras something to aspire to." The boys like me, but they think of me as living in another world, one they'll never enter and probably don't even want to enter. Consequently, they can't take me too seriously. I can conceive of a time when it would be best for me to bow to men like Josh and Paul and step aside and walk away.

But that time has not come; and it may not come at all. These two men may be the *only* qualified Negroes who come to us from outside the ghetto. Certainly, most of the middle-class Negroes in Charleston stay as far away from the slum areas as possible. And after all, it is more the responsibility of white people in this town than it is of Negroes in New York to break the cycle of our Charleston ghettos. There's one other point that needs to be made. If we let the Joshes and the Pauls do all our work for us, even if they are successful, we will be cheating ourselves. The Negro is growing up. If we white folks will help, we will grow up too. We can help them learn to stand erect; they can help us learn the meaning of life itself. There are big dances in Charleston every week of the year.

Yesterday, we lost Freddie; last night and today, we were given encouraging signs of new life. In the words of Mrs. Martin, "The Lord taketh away, but then, before you know it, the Lord giveth back."

August 2. Racing against time, Mrs. Gray and I continue our search for the four missing fathers. Our investigation is at once absurd, disappointing, and illuminating.

We are trying to find the four men but hoping all the while that we will have no success. If we don't find them, Mrs. Gray stands a chance of receiving aid. If we do find them, she will once again have to depend on men who had already proven their complete unreliability. So we are looking; but then again, we are not looking. Don't you hate to get mixed up with the government?

Touring darkest Charleston is like descending to the center of the earth. Most of the places we visited were up back alleys, places where there is no grass, no color. Everything is a dirt brown. I write out the statements for the people to sign, and do most of the talking. Mrs. Gray introduces me around. The only thing we could get on one husband, a "passing friend" of Mrs. Gray's was this: "It is said that Alston Calvin's mother once lived here. We have heard that his mother died; and we have never seen Alston Calvin." It took me no little while to word that statement correctly. Alston Calvin is not listed in any directory. The only thing Mrs. Gray knows about him is that his mother once lived at the address we visited. The present occupants, a man and a woman, who yell at each other loud enough to scare a white boy off, once knew the mother but did not know for sure that she lived in their apartment.

And then there was that woman who lives in the house in front of Mrs. Gray, who at first refused to sign. Mrs. Gray had asked her for her signature yesterday but this woman said that she was not going to put her name *anywhere* even though she had not seen any of the husbands. This afternoon when I went with Mrs. Gray to see her again, she was leaning back in a wooden chair outside of her apartment door. Her hair was long and uncombed. The bottom two or three buttons of her shirt were undone. Her navel was showing. She must have been in her fifties.

"Mary Belle," she said, as we approached, "I told you I wasn't going to put my name to that thing."

"Please reconsider, your signature is one that we really need." I was speaking.

"Oh you do, do you? Well, how is it that no one helped me out when my boy drowned in Colonial Lake?"

"I'm sorry to hear that."

"Ye-ar, well I'm sorry too."

"Mrs. Gray said that you haven't seen any of the four men. All we want you to do is to sign your name stating . . ."

"And have some white man come banging on my door. I ain't about to put my name to that thing."

"Look, it's not for me. It's not even for Mrs. Gray. It's for her children. I give you my word that no one will bother you.

I work right around the corner at St. Paul's and if anyone should give you a hard time, I'll come give you a hand right away. Please . . ."

"I don't like it."

I took a deep breath and argued and argued and begged and begged until, finally, she signed.

In the onetime neighborhood of husband number three, Mrs. Gray introduced me to an old, old woman who had something of a goatee and pure white hair. "Mary Belle," she said, "you've had a hard time. I know you have. I'll pray to Jesus that you get some help this time." Since she couldn't sign her name, she made an "x," which I witnessed and which I took to the center for Linda to witness.

On the way back, we saw Mrs. Gray's son Edward walking along slowly, carrying an armful of soda bottles; so we stopped and gave him a ride to Mr. Dick's that he might cash them in.

August 3. Mrs. Gray and I do some of our work over the telephone. There is a man in the phone book with the same name as husband number one. She called to ask this man if he was the one who fathered her oldest girl . . . and hung up quickly when a white man on the other end of the line answered. I have been trying to get in touch with the Negro rental agent who is the previous landlord of husband number three; but somehow I "just miss" him each time I call. The secretary is getting tired of my calling but is unable to tell me why the rental agent hasn't returned any of my calls.

Now that Father Andrews is away, one of my duties is to dispense the money. Since I'm setting aside the full amount of the discretionary fund, $35, for Mrs. Gray, I find this duty

very simple. I just say, "No." About eleven today, a certain
Rosa Simmons came to see me about a "loan." She is of average height and age, but her rump is as big as a backyard wash-
tub. She brought several little children with her, all of them
naked from the waist up. Also with her was a legal document
that she left with me, a notice of eviction, which she said
would take place today if she didn't pay the rent. Like all
rents in this neighborhood, it is $25 a month. She said that
she had been sick and had to quit work and that it would be
three weeks before she could draw unemployment. And she
just had to get that $25.

I told her the financial situation I was in, but we talked for
some time anyway. She was very interesting to me; I'm not
sure how I impressed her. She's the prototype of this matriarchal culture, the mother who endures, who, against all odds,
raises her many children to maturity. How would the people
of my night world respond if someone was about to put them
out on the sidewalk? I'm positive I would contemplate suicide. But not Rosa. She's used to this sort of thing. She's
beat all those people before, rent collectors, loan swindlers,
constables; and she'll beat them again. She has the problems
of Mrs. Gray but the wiles of a cat and the composition of a
rock. For example, she has her fourteen-year-old girl working
in the fields this summer at $7 a day. Now as Rosa says: "It's
good for dat chile to work; but better'n that, next summer she
can draw unemployment in the little town near where she's
been working."

"Is that right? They pay unemployment to a kid that age?"

"Sho, man. And besides that, I can send her to get a job as a
clean-up girl somewhere in Charleston while she draws dat
unemployment pay."

No, they won't get Rosa. I sent her on to Sister Margaret and told her, before she left, that if those people actually start moving her out to the sidewalk, to call me and I'd be right there. But I don't expect to hear from her.

Later today while Josh and Paul were having a meeting with the Boys Club, Sally, the Head Start director, and I struck up a conversation with Mitchell, a Negro about seventeen, who was sent to us by the Neighborhood Youth Corps. Sally is upset because Mitchell hasn't been doing any janitorial work around the place. She thinks *she* is supposed to be Mitchell's boss, but she isn't sure. Maybe Adam is. Maybe I am. Probably the only person who knows for sure is some clerk up in Washington. Sally and I thought we would approach Mitchell using what we call "the subtle approach." He was out on the porch, whittling a piece of wood, near where we were sitting, playing a game of Scrabble. "Say, Mitchell, what does your job description call for?" Sally asked, making a three-letter word.

"Oh, you know, I'm supposed to keep the place clean and play with the little children."

"Are you supposed to clean up? I didn't know that," I interrupted.

"Ye-ar but I been slackin' off. You see, I haven't been able to hold a check for the last month. The lawyer takes it all."

"Is that right? What for?"

"Well, you see, they are trying to say I got into some trouble with the Jackson Street Panthers; and I'm out on a thousand dollars' bond."

"Really," I said, as I made the word "run." "What kind of trouble, Mitchell?"

"Well, you see, they say some of those fellows killed a white taxicab driver." He paused to blow some bits of wood off his knife. "But I didn't have anything to do with it. They picked me up just 'cause I look like someone else."

"Really?"

"Yep, those fellows get in all kinds of trouble. This is the fourth person they've been accused of killing. I stay away from them. The police picked me up because I let my hair grow long; but after that, my mother made me cut it short."

"Really?"

"Yep, I believe I'll go downtown this afternoon and talk to my lawyer."

"You want to see how your case is coming along?" Sally asked, rather anxiously.

"No, man, I'm not worried about that. I want to see if I can hold one of my checks."

So life goes on.

August 4. Since nothing much happened at the center today, I will take this opportunity to report a conversation I had the other day with a friend of the family, a lady "up in years," a person very dear to me, one who knows about hardship herself. I went to see her to tell her about how I was writing a diary this summer, how I had sent a copy of this diary to an editor friend of mine at Houghton Mifflin, and how this editor friend was very encouraging about eventual publication.

My friend did most of the talking, slowly and with concern. I, for a change, listened to her. "I can tell that you feel compelled to write this thing, but why? . . . It certainly is a bad time to have something like this published, what with all the cry for 'Black Power.' . . . It seems so hard that you have to use your writing ability for something so, as you say, 'controversial.' . . . We have had such peaceful integration and good feelings here in Charleston. What could all this gain? Could it stir up real trouble with our fellow colored people? . . . William, I don't want you to get hurt, that's my main concern. You're an idealist, you know. You have deep thinking and feeling but so little experience in this hard world. . . . But whatever you do, I want you to know that I am with you."

I didn't know what to say then; I don't know what to say now.

August 5. The trouble with us idealists is that when we get down and disillusioned, we tend to fall apart. After completing my work on Mrs. Gray's case, I called a young lawyer for advice in the event that we lose the case. He said that he would do anything in his power to help and also suggested that I call one of the workers at the Welfare Department, whom he knows and likes and who has some position of authority. This lady, whom I did call, sounded about my mother's age over the telephone. I spoke of the difficulties and absurdities I had run into in Mrs. Gray's case and pointed out what seemed to me to be the flaws in our welfare system. She countered with good points of her own.

It was the classic argument between the young idealist who wants to save the world and runs the risk of saving no one, including himself, and the experienced realist who does a single job and does it well. She told me that she had been working in this department many years and had seen countless Mary Belle Grays. I had become involved in only one case. She said that her department had very limited funds and could not support everyone. Furthermore, when a mother such as Mrs. Gray with four husbands to father six children comes for aid, such an apparently irresponsible person cannot take priority over a mother with fewer children and fewer men. Welfare aid must be distributed where it can be used most responsibly.

"But what about those six children, are you going to let them starve?" I asked. That of course, made her plenty mad and for good reason. She didn't cause anyone to starve. She was just doing her job the best way possible with the funds available. How would you like to decide which families to save and which not to save? she seemed to be saying.

And then she struck at me, inferring that I was the type of do-gooder who is trying to assert deficient ego by feeling sorry for the indigent like Mrs. Gray. I let it pass, but that remark hurt. She has something on me. She is not the first person who has told me that — and it always hurts. But you know, I believe a good psychiatrist could find ulterior and unlovely motives behind what anyone does. The point is, there is a need to be met in our city, a desperate need, and someone, whether he be deficient of ego or overendowed with ego, must try to meet that need. Right? Right.

Then she briefly explained her philosophy of work with the poor. She thinks it is vitally important to get the husbands and fathers to support the children and to get the mothers accustomed to the idea of working for themselves. I told her that I was as much for the Negro standing up and making his own way as she was but that, in this particular case, welfare may be the only hope of keeping those six children alive. Even if Mrs. Gray is able to go back to work, it will mean that the older children will have to stay home from school to mind the younger children. Thus, all six will be grossly neglected. If society doesn't help one family now, I went on, it may have to support seven families in twenty years.

She answered by talking again about my having seen only one case, and the countless numbers of such cases she sees all the time. I asked her if she would cooperate if we set up a volunteer organization to help people like Mrs. Gray gather statements and go to the court. Her answer to me was a puzzling one. "No," she said emphatically, "you leave these people to us."

There's nothing deficient about *her* ego, I thought to myself. We talked a little longer; and I told her that I was an idealist — she agreed — and that, you know, I'm going to hang on to those ideals until our society does something about its starving children. We wished each other pleasant goodbyes.

So it sounds as though Mrs. Gray was defeated before she started, that another family, "more worthy," will use the limited funds of the Welfare Department. I was fighting over nothing. What will happen to the family now? What will happen to me now? Ego-deficient! What right has she to call me that! What will become of Black-y-mo? Yes, I got awfully down. I thought I had overcome my personal problem of depression but this is at least as bad as before.

But then again, when we idealists are up, we are *really* up. We feel great. We can almost say that God's in his heaven and all's right with the world. I wrote the first part of the entry for August fifth in the seclusion of Father Andrews' air-conditioned office earlier in the afternoon. Since that time, the wife and the mother of the young lawyer who is helping me have called and expressed their interest and concern in Mrs. Gray's case. But even more important, Josh and Paul showed up at five o'clock with six bags of groceries, clothing, and supplies. They had spent all day raising money in their squadrons at the Air Base. Also, they plan to get to know the Grays and, over a period of time, help them to help themselves. The problem is by no means solved, but that people are working for a solution makes things seem not quite so bad. In fact, while I sit here in this office and type, listening to Josh and Paul drill the boys — "Dress Right, Dress, Rea-a-a-a-a-ady, Front" — I begin to feel downright good.

As long as there are men like Josh and Paul in the world, we idealists stand a chance. When we are disillusioned, we suffer, we hurt, we fall apart; but if we are able to hang on, able to get out of bed the next morning, out of the pit of despair, and report to work as usual — before you know it — some sympathetic lawyer's mother, some Josh or Paul will appear on the scene; and once again this becomes a good world to live in. Thank you, Lord.

August 6. No entry.

August 7. Sunday afternoon. We've just returned from our overnight camping trip, the one Freddie helped us plan. We went to a place that Linda and I discovered two or three weeks ago when we took the little fellows and girls on the outing. Located twenty miles from Charleston, at least two miles from the nearest house, on a deep saltwater creek, the picnic and camping area is owned by a large paper company. The sign says:

WELCOME

ENJOY YOUR OUTING

Courtesy
International Paper Company

With a name like that, Linda and I were sure that even our boys would be welcome. My mother, however, didn't like the idea at all. She wasn't worried about the paper company so much; but she said, "That's in Hell-Hole Swamp, William; you know how those country people out there feel about the Nigras." "They hate them," my father answered for me. "And they are apt to make serious trouble for you if you take some out there to spend the night," my mother continued. But since Linda and I hardly saw an automobile when we were there before, I decided to take a chance and have the overnight trip there anyway.

This camping trip took quite a bit of preparation. I went to see the mother of each boy. I think they are getting used to me in the St. Paul's neighborhood, because all were friendly except for Sneed's mother. She really despises me. "No, I ain' lettin' him go. I ain' goin' to let him go nowhere with you."

"Don't pay her no mind, Mr. Barnwell," Sneed told me later. "My pappy will let me go." And he did.

I looked up Teet, who seldom comes to the center these days, to see if he wanted to join us. He giggled a little when I was speaking to him. Though he said he would like to go on the trip, he did not show up yesterday morning at the appointed hour.

Yesterday was an unusually cool day for Charleston summer. Florence's sewing class (which, by the way, is flourishing) came outside to wish us good-bye. Paul and Josh were not able to go, but Kinloch Manigault (pronounced Kinlaw Manigo), a young Negro man who has recently returned home from the service, joined us. On the trip down, we passed the place where I killed my one and only deer. I was right at the age of these boys when I killed him. In this part of the country, there is an ancient custom that when you make your first kill, the other hunters smear the deer's blood all over you and won't let you wash it off before you return home. I can still remember how my mother screamed when she met me at the door. I hope there's no blood shed on this trip, I thought to myself grimly, as we drove along.

When we arrived, Kinloch made the boys clean up the camp and pitch the tent. Then he took them on a five-mile hike while I lay down in the tent and dozed, delighted that Kinloch had come along. I was awakened by a pick-up truck that pulled off the road into the camping area. I was relieved when I saw that a Negro was driving the truck, joyous when I recognized him. It was Shem, the porter at the bank where I used to work. We sat down and had a grand time talking about our bank. He gave me the latest inside news on all my old friends. Shem said that he lived not too far away and that he was out in his truck in search of fishing worms. I think he suspected that I was nervous about trouble from the local toughs because he said to me right before he left, "You know where I live now. If you run into any difficulty, just come up the road and stay with me. Old Shem is always there."

On returning, Kinloch and the boys took their shoes off, baited their lines, and once again fell to their favorite sport — crabbing. They caught twenty-four, and when we cooked supper we saved our crab-crakkin for dessert. After we finished eating, it was time for me to tell them ghost stories and then send them to bed. The tent was large enough for everyone, even for me; but I slept in the car. When I thought about sleeping all night in that badly ventilated tent with those ten crab-cracking scouts, I decided that this is where my racial liberalism ends. They went to sleep right away; I sat up poking the fire for two or three hours before I turned in — just poking the fire, smoking and thinking.

I was by myself now, away from whites and blacks, welfare workers and Mary Belle Grays. It was not the "nigger-hating" country boys who live in Hell-Hole Swamp that I was afraid of. It certainly was not the ghouls and other ghosts I had invoked from the burning embers for the boys a short while before. But out there in the silence of the woods, in the darkness of the night, I was afraid. It was not the kind of fear I imagine a man feels when he's engaged in combat, when he's facing possible death. Rather, it was more the fear of the boy at prep school who wakes up in the middle of the night and wants his mother and father, but dares not cry lest his roommate hear him; or the fear of the sophomore in college who sits up all night by himself studying for an exam and suddenly discovers that life has dimensions to it that he never before dreamed of; or the fear of the young ensign who stands his first night watch as OOD underway and, looking out from the bridge at the vast, turbulent sea, wonders what in the world he's doing there. Am I letting myself become too involved in this difficult question of race relations? What is the ultimate meaning of all this, anyway? If I am fighting against the world that raised me, whom can I run to for comfort now? Alone in the stillness of the night.

But then I got sleepy too and made my bed on the back seat of the car and was soon free from fear and dreaming pretty dreams of blue castles far away.

At six o'clock, we were all up, cooking breakfast, crabbing, hiking, cleaning up the site. We left at eleven. I was quite pleased with the way the Boys Club handled themselves on their first overnight. Maybe these fellows were hard to organize at first; but now they respond quite well to the scouting objectives, the athletic instruction, the military drill, and, on occasion, the worship services. Like Florence's sewing class, they began slowly but are now moving right alone. I realize, of course, that without Freddie, Josh, and now Kinloch, I wouldn't have gotten very far with them.

Several white people drove by us this morning before we left. None stopped; but as they passed by, the drivers almost broke their necks looking back around at us, especially when they saw me. We looked back at them the same way, the damn crackers. The camping site was cleaner when we left than it was when we arrived.

My wife met me at the door this time. There wasn't a drop of blood on me; but oh, I was dirty. She screamed at me as loudly as my mother had screamed, fifteen years ago.

VII

Of Bread and of Love

Well, friends, this time I don't care; I'm going out and get stewed tonight myself. I'm tired of feeling guilty. Like Sally, I have done my work well — and so to hell with them. It sounds as though Brian is right after all: "They can live their lives; I'll live mine." And I know how to handle that guilt that drove me to the ghetto in the first place. . . .

It's too bad the summer didn't end the night of the big dance; but I guess that's life.

◑

Then Jesus was led up by the
Spirit into the wilderness to be
tempted by the devil. And he fasted
forty days and forty nights, and
afterward he was hungry. And the
tempter came and said to him, "If you
are the Son of God, command these
stones to become loaves of bread."
But he answered, "It is written,

'Man shall not live by bread alone,
but by every word that proceeds
from the mouth of God.' "

— St. Matthew

AUGUST 8. Well, I'm all clean and slicked up now. Father Andrews suggested before he left that I break down and wear a coat and tie while I'm in charge this month. That, and sitting in his office at the desk, would help to give me the image of authority I need. So here I sit this Monday morning, watching the life of the ghetto pass by outside the large window of my new air-conditioned office and with the top two buttons of my Dacron coat fastened. Father Andrews is right. Already, I can tell that my authority is respected. If someone is hitting someone else over the head with a pool cue, all I have to do is to open the door and bellow out in my deepest voice to "stop that foolishness." And the trouble stops — usually.

For the first time since the beginning of the summer, I find myself without anything much to do. The Boys Club, the sewing class are well taken care of. Mrs. Gray and I have done all that we can do for the time being. Linda and I are planning to form a girls' club but cannot do any more work on that project until we find someone to take charge of it. Sally has the Head Start program fairly well organized and does not need my help. Adam, Michael, Kinloch, and Mitchell are keeping the place clean. Mrs. Martin says she has Black-y-mo "straightened out," which means that he's learning not to beat on the little girls even though the big boys beat on him.

So, sitting here, I ask myself, what should I be doing? More particularly, I am wondering what I, as a seminarian, *should* be doing? How does my role differ from that of the social worker? What is the unique role of the church in this neighborhood? My question is one that seminarians struggle with constantly. What is the unique role of the church in the life of the non-church, twentieth-century world?

I feel that the church has two functions. On the one hand, it must simply *be*. On the other, it must *act*. Jesus first called to him the twelve and then — sent them out two by two. The church fulfills its first function by answering Jesus' call to come unto him. Through its worship, its meeting together, its book, the church develops a self-consciousness. It becomes a people in the same way that Israel is a people. The church fulfills its second function by going out into the world, two by two. And in going out into the world, the church follows Jesus, Jesus who listened to the world, Jesus who gave up his life for the world.

The being of the church is the church standing up, growing into self-consciousness; the acting of the church is the church laying down its life for its friends; dying, if necessary, to its self-consciousness. In seminary and church circles, there are some who say that the church in its many worldly activities — in hospitals, in industrial plants, in mission centers like St. Paul's, in civil rights demonstrations — is losing its sense of being. And they say that when its sense of being is lost, its knowledge of the Transcendent God, in whom the church is centered, will be lost. There are others who say that the church, the parish church in particular, is so concerned with its own being and self-perpetuation that it is not going out into the world, is not acting. Rather, it is building larger and larger churches and seeking to glorify itself more and more. And if it continues to glorify itself, its knowledge of the Transcendent God, who is outside of the church, will be lost. Both sets of critics are right.

And if the church does not listen continuously to both, it will become completely identified with the world, or it will build modern Towers of Babel.

This summer, in my work here at the center, I have been engaged primarily in the acting function of the church. I have been ready to give up my church consciousness in order to fulfill my duties in the world, ready to replace the worship service with boxing practice, ready to take the boys on overnight trips rather than go to church on Sunday. I still *feel* like a Christian; but if I continue to move further and further away from the people who consciously answer Jesus' call to come unto him, I will be apt to lose my knowledge of, my identity in the Transcendent God.

The church is like the director of St. Paul's Mission Center. It must go outside where there are people playing pool, where there are little girls doing handstands, where two boys are now arguing over a Pepsi-Cola bottle. But it must also dress itself in a coat and tie, sit in an enclosed office, bellow out in its deepest voice at the world on the other side of the window glass.

The director must maintain himself as an authority; he must be ready to give up all authority in order to listen to and help the people with whom he is charged.

August 9. I like being an authority; and I like being in the office. It's cool in here. The more I stay in the office, the more of an authority I will be. Yesterday, I maintained my authority by staying in the office and writing about the church in the world. Today, I will do the same thing, except today, I will write about the government in the world. More particularly, I will write about the government anti-poverty programs here at the center.

My general thinking in regard to these programs is that when a community does not meet its own needs, either because of a lack of concern or because of a lack of resources, government anti-poverty spending becomes necessary. I do think, however, that we must be very careful in our promotion of these programs, not because they aren't good, but because they make us forget our individual responsibility to other individuals in society. In the past, it has been too easy for me to vote for big government and forget about people like Mrs. Gray and retarded Richard. Now they are a part of my life. Even as I write this, Richard is ever before me. He is, in fact, watching me through the window of the office right now. Only the top half of his face is visible. His nose is slightly squashed against the glass pane; his black and white eyes follow my every movement . . .

I've mentioned before that we have here at the center a Head Start program for about thirty kindergarten-age children as well as a Job Corps recruiting office. Also, we take two or three high school dropouts from the Neighborhood Youth Corps. In spite of the fact that I know all the staff and most of the children and teen-agers involved in these programs, I know very little about the internal structure of the programs themselves.

Head Start seems to be doing the most good. Every day I see five-year-old kids singing songs, dancing "this way and that way" to records, making long trains of themselves by holding on to the fellow in front. It is true that the little boys make a god-awful mess of the only men's rooms as they learn to stand rather than sit. But then you go outside and watch them acting out "London Bridge" and the men's room doesn't matter so much. The children are building up their vocabulary, learning how to work and play with other kids, and above all they are receiving adult guidance and attention from both Negro and white.

Sally seems to be doing an excellent job as temporary supervisor of the program. She is more or less in charge of two Head Start teachers, three assistants, and of Adam, Michael, Mitchell, and Kinloch. In addition to doing her job with the children — and doing it efficiently and sensitively — Sally is strong when it comes to dealing with the staff. When Michael isn't doing his job properly, it is easy to say, "Well, that's all right. After all what do you expect? He never had a chance in life." That kind of thinking does neither the program nor Michael any good. And Sally doesn't let her sensitivity to the oppressed stand in the way of getting the job done. If it means pushing people like Michael harder than they are accustomed to being pushed, she'll push them. I am told that the Head Start program requires the usual amount of government reports and back-up and paper work, which is a shame because it takes too much time away from people like Sally.

I had one encounter with the Job Corps this summer. Linda, who takes care of all the work for this, got sick, and I was left for several days to do the best I could with her job. I interviewed some young men who were undecided about joining, some who were sent to us by police probation officers, some

who definitely wanted to join. All I could tell these young
men about the program was what I've heard from others who
have been away for training and who have returned. Most, I
think, have thought the experience profitable, but it is rather
difficult to tell. I get mostly "yes" and "no" answers from
them. One fellow was very enthusiastic about the heavy farm
equipment training that he'd received but was discouraged
when he couldn't find a job in the Charleston area. Another
was forced to return home early because someone hit him on
the head with a shovel.

One thing really surprised me about the local recruits for
the Job Corps. A good many whites have applied and been
accepted through our office. People always say that the whites
who come from the lower classes in the South, and in this area
in particular, are the ones who really hate the Negroes. "They
hate them because the only thing they have that the Negroes
don't have is white skin." There may be much truth in that
statement, but I've seen many exceptions. Yesterday, for example, I was talking with a white woman and her son who
come from a small farm on one of the islands south of
Charleston. I found out that it had been their Negro friends
who had told them about the Job Corps and sent them to see
me. About three weeks ago, I struck up a conversation with a
young white man who had been to a Job Corps training station and had returned after his period of obligation expired.
He complained about the fighting and the stealing but said
that he hadn't minded the mixing of the races at all. "It's not
much different from home," he said, probably thinking of the
many times he had helped harvest crops with Negroes. And
then, I see other white boys who come to the center to sign
up, and I see them playing pool with the fellows here and kid-

ding them, and taking kidding in return. All of which tells me that on this difficult question of race, it is better to see for yourself what people really do and think than it is to believe only what you read and hear. My night world people would love you to think that all the trouble comes from the lower classes. And I will have to admit that in my description of the overnight trip in Hell-Hole Swamp, I was trying to make you think that too.

Richard left during my reflections on the Job Corps. He's back at the window for our last anti-poverty program, the Neighborhood Youth Corps. From this organization, we have been sent, during the course of the summer, three young Negro men and two white girls. I didn't get to know the first fellow who came; he only stayed a few days. The second one was a long-haired Jackson Street Panther who had little to say and who, one day, just quit coming. The third is Mitchell who, in spite of the fact that he can't hold his check, has been doing a better job of cleaning up. We are supposed to train him in something besides janitorial work, but we simply don't have the staff to do this. What would we train him in anyway? The two white girls were assigned to work directly under the Head Start supervisor. Like the Job Corps recruits, they worked well in this integrated situation. But one of the girls got pregnant, and when she began to show, the government people had to take her off the program, though they did help her find a place in a home for unwed mothers. When she left, the other girl left in loyalty to her. At least that's why we think she left; she never would say.

From the side of the anti-poverty program that I see, I am positive that the government is accomplishing at least some of what it set out to do — help the beaten down in society to stand up, provide channels whereby the oppressed can receive love and discipline. It is too bad that this community has not done anything much to meet its own needs and that the federal government has had to step in in such force. Only the Roman Catholics are making a significant effort. This summer, for example, they brought in thirteen nuns from Minnesota to teach ghetto kids in a special summer school.

My night world people really have little room to criticize big government and "that s.o.b. in the White House" when it is their lack of good citizenship that created the void which the government is trying to fill.

Right, Richard? Right.

Nuts! My image of authority has been crushed. I might as well take off my coat and tie and go outside again. A few days ago, I wrote about Rosa with the large rump. I delighted in the fact that she had beaten rent collectors, loan swindlers, and constables before and that she would beat them again. Little did I realize that while we talked she was laying the groundwork to beat me. Today, she sent in the fourteen-year-old girl, a sweet kid with big eyes and a warm smile, to tell me that if I could lend her mother only nine dollars, she could get the rest from an uncle. I wrote out the check on my own account.

But worse than the loss of the nine dollars was the pride I had to swallow when a certain Negro woman, a Mrs. Calvin, called up and said that Father Andrews had asked her to do volunteer work at the center and that, since she had the free time, she would like to begin.

"That's great," I said. "We were looking for someone to set

up a program for the young girls. Could you work with them?"

"I can work with *any* age, you see, that's my job during the year."

"Well, that's great, we sure can use you around here."

"YOU can use me! I'm accustomed to programming cirricula for schools and churches and you say YOU can use me."

Tyrant! Nigger tyrant! "Well, excuse me, I didn't mean it that way. I only meant that the children do need someone of your caliber to direct them."

"Well, all right. I'll be there tomorrow at three."

What do you mean, bossing me around? Am I not in charge? Am I not the authority here? Tyrant. "Good-bye now, look forward to seeing you at three."

August 10. Something happened today which leaves me wondering whether I should be proud and fight back or be humble and beg forgiveness.

It was late in the afternoon, after Josh had spent another very successful two hours with the boys. I was giving him a ride back to the Air Base. We were chatting about the work at the center and his work in the military. And then, abruptly changing the subject, he turned to me and said, "We're having a party at — Church Street, Saturday night. I'd like you to come to it."

"Sorry," I said without hesitation, "but I'm tied up." "Sorry" and "tied up" were good words for my state when Josh, the guy who has given me as much hope this summer as anyone, asked me to an integrated party to be held in a white neighborhood, four or five blocks from where my parents live.

So you'd like me to come to your party, how nice! . . . We

were getting along so well, why did you . . . Nigger . . .
why did you have to ruin it so soon with that inevitable invitation; or was it more of an ultimatum? . . . I've got my own
social life you know, I can't be expected to give my nights as
well as my days to your cause. . . . Josh, old fellow, I'd really
like to come; but you see it's a question of strategy. Don't you
think it would hurt our fight in the long run if I were. . . .
What would my parents think? They've got to be considered.
They *are* my parents, you. . . . Man, come clean, you don't
want me to come to your party, you're testing me, you. . . . I
know I sound phony, but honest to God, I'm not. I've been
working hard as hell this summer, haven't I, haven't I? And I
tell you something else, I've been to lots of integrated parties
in Washington, but down here it's just. . . . Nigger. . . .
Look Josh, if it were a question of one party that would be
one thing, but I can't afford to start setting *precedents*.

"By the way," I asked without changing my expression or
voice, "how long have you been in the Air Force?"

I don't remember what Josh said, but I do remember that
he gave only "yes" and "no" answers to my other questions during the rest of the ride. He had met my kind before, or so he
thought — "tied up" and "sorry."

I didn't talk with Josh about my prejudice, which is there
whether I like it or not, my honest skepticism about my going
to the party, or my anger at his putting me on the spot. But
here in the junk room in this blessed attic fan breeze, I'm feeling more and more like fighting, not crying.

The trouble with the world is that everyone wants you to
hate yourself. The welfare woman wants me to hate myself
for being a do-gooder, my night world wants me to hate myself

for being an integrationist, and now Josh wants me to hate myself for being a segregationist.

Well, to tell you the truth, I'm glad I said no to his invitation. Maybe I'm not ready to "lay down my life"; and I'll tell you something else, if I ever do, I want it to be my decision, not that of someone else, especially not that of some. . . . I said earlier in the summer that the Negro would have to stand up and fight his own battle. Well, there comes a time when we white folks have to stand up and fight back. My general rule this summer on integration is this: I will accept and promote any type of integration if it is for the purpose of giving the Negro children a chance in life. I offered to go down to the YMCA with Josh to argue with them about their segregation practices; but I didn't want to go to Josh's party, and I could not see how my going would make any difference to the kids at the center. It would have been integration simply for the sake of integration. And that, I do not accept. I would have been even phonier if I had gone; if indeed I am phony at all.

I made one exception to my rule on integration this summer. Adam told me one day that he was going to have a little party at his house for a few friends and "you are invited." I accepted that invitation and, furthermore, I was proud that I had been asked. Adam was not testing me. When I told him that I could not return the invitation because we were living with my parents, he shrugged it off. "I see what you mean," he said. Adam, wise and loyal Adam, knew what I meant. When Adam asked me to his party, I knew that my accepting would not improve my work at the center — he and I talk most every day over a beer anyway — but I accepted because I really wanted to go; I wanted to know Adam and his wife in their small home, which I found was, on the inside, worlds removed from the peeling paint and rotting wood on the outside. I had a reason for accepting Adam's invitation; our friendship has grown slowly but deeply this summer. It was not to help my fight to give the boys a chance; nor was it integration only for the sake of integration. It was simply going to the party of a friend.

"William," my wife said, when she finished reading this, "you've made it sound like you actually went to Adam's party."

"But. . . ."

"I know you accepted and I know you visited him at his home. . . ."

"But the point is. . . ."

"But the point is, you didn't go to the party, and if you don't change this, you'll be *using* Adam. What if he ever reads this thing? How do you think *he* will feel about it?"

"But. . . ."

You've ruined the whole entry, you realize that don't you!

August 11. I'm becoming more and more anxious for my job to end. Early in the summer, I was worried about my motives for wanting to work at St. Paul's. Now, I need to examine my reasons for wanting to leave. If it were in my power to work beyond the 26th of August, would I be right to quit? Or should I stay on? Here are some of my reasons for wanting to leave:

I'm not as energetic as before. It was not until I sat down to rest in this air-conditioned office that I realized how tired, physically and emotionally, I am. How much of my fatigue is laziness? How much is real exhaustion?

I'm not as much needed as before. Josh and Paul are doing a better job with the boys than I ever did. And they are not alone. They themselves have brought some of their friends to help; and yesterday, Mrs. Calvin started the Girls Club with about twenty anxious members. The girls elected officers, planned some trips, and have already begun their handicraft work. Since their meeting, they have been talking continuously about their club, telling me how much better it is than the "stupid old Boys Club." With Paul and Josh working with the boys, and Mrs. Calvin working with the girls, I have little to do.

On the overnight trip, the boys made up a chant about how they were Barnwell Wildcats and Barnwell Panthers; and of course I've been calling them "my" boys all summer. Those days are over. The time has come when I must drop the adjective, "my," at least with that particular group. They are Josh's boys now and hopefully, under his keen supervision, will soon become young men. But am I really no longer needed?

I'm not as much liked or respected as before. Josh was very indifferent to me today, though he has not let his personal feelings interfere with our work together, with our struggle to help give the kids a chance in life. And this Mrs. Calvin, while she is pleasant now, still gives me the impression that she thinks I don't belong here. And finally, yesterday and to-day — in spite of the fact that I've worn my tie — Adam and Michael have not responded to my requests that they clean the place up properly. Should I let this lack of popularity, this lack of authority affect my decision as to whether or not to keep working?

I don't feel as energetic, as needed, or as popular as before. Moreover, the initial thrill of entering the Negro culture is over. I'm finding myself spending most of the day in the office.

It could be that now is the time to step aside and to allow for the growth of the ghetto. But then again, it could be that now is the very time when I should work my hardest, a time when there is no one to encourage me, a time when there is little joy in my work.

August 12. When I wrote the entry yesterday, I was thinking of the possibility of a fairly gradual and undramatic break with the mission center and with the Negroes of the ghetto. I did not foresee what would happen today. Today was the last day of Sally's summer employment. It was also the day that Adam and Michael turned against the white staff — Linda, Sally, and me.

It all started this morning when Linda gave Adam and Michael the keys to drive her car up to the hose where it could be washed. Instead — without drivers' licenses — they drove away and didn't reappear for two hours. I wasn't at the center at the time, but Linda told me later that she was frantic. She had already collected insurance for an accident which was her fault; and these boys don't know how to drive, not really. When they did return, Adam, at first, denied that he had ever been in the car. But Linda knew better and gave them both hell. Michael growled at her and began to sulk. Then they went out and started drinking. A couple of hours passed. I was back now, not paying too much attention to what had happened, sitting in the office, fiddling around.

They came back and, this time, Michael began expressing his hostility toward Sally, not Linda. After all, it was Sally who had pushed him so hard this summer. Now that he was striking back at one of the white staff members, he might as well get even with her at the same time. He told her what a lousy job she had done, how he would be glad to see her go, and lastly, "Please for God's sake, white boss lady, don't ever come back here again." Adam, wise and loyal Adam, stood by silent. By this time, I was outside and found myself defending Sally, telling Michael that he didn't know who his friends were, that if he were truly loyal to the center, as everyone says he is, he would know and appreciate what a good job Sally has done with the five-year-olds from this neighborhood. My interference only egged Michael on. Adam stood by, silent. Silent. Then Sally shook hands with those of us who would shake her hand and walked toward the car — slowly — amidst cries of "Bye, white boss lady, bye, bye."

If Adam and Michael are the leaders in this community that everyone says they are, you begin to know how much chance you have in your effort to help the rest of the neighborhood help themselves.

Well, friends, this time I don't care; I'm going out and get stewed tonight myself. I'm tired of feeling guilty. Like Sally, I have done my work well — and so to hell with them. It sounds as though Brian is right after all: "They can live their lives; I'll live mine." And I know how to handle that guilt that drove me to the ghetto in the first place. When I finish seminary, I'll find me a nice little wealthy church in distant suburbia, pay my maid a decent salary, vote for liberal Democrats, discuss the race problem over whiskey sours and pickled shrimp — while I send my children to private schools, buy myself a great big, long-haired dog and my wife a color TV, and to hell with the ghetto Negro. I mean it! To hell with him. Monday, I'm going to tell them that this is their community center, "Run it boys, you want it, take it, good luck." Me, I'm going to lock myself in the office until the 26th.

It's too bad that the summer didn't end the night of the big dance; but I guess that's life.

August 13. Well, I can say this morning that it's a good thing the summer didn't end last night either. I didn't get stewed after all. Instead, my wife dragged me out to see *Who's Afraid of Virginia Woolf.* (God, I thought I had problems.) That helped me take my mind off myself; but the thing that is really helping me rethink my connection with the ghetto is the fact that I'm trying to write a sermon about Mr. Freddie to preach tomorrow at Father Andrews's church. I'm not going to sit here at this typewriter and say that yesterday I was wrong to stand up for Sally and wrong to stand up for myself. I should probably have been harder on Michael and Adam than I was. But I *will* say this: Standing up and asserting yourself is not the whole story. A man must be a man, but a man also must learn to love. And this morning, while I sit here struggling to write my sermon on Freddie, it's about love that I'm thinking:

> And Jesus sat down opposite the treasury and watched the multitude putting money into the treasury. Many rich people put in large sums. And a poor widow came, and put in two copper coins, which make a penny. And Jesus called his dis-

*ciples to him and said to them, "Truly, I say to you, this poor
widow has put in more than all those who are contributing to
the treasury. For they all contributed out of their abundance;
but she out of her poverty has put in everything she had, her
whole living."*

One month ago there was a young man from the Negro community named Freddie. He was a short fellow with a little moustache,
a big smile, and a brace around his wrist to keep a broken bone in
place. Freddie was twenty-six and had never held a regular job.
You see, he had a bad heart condition. Ever since he was a little
boy, he had been real sick. Some say he spent half of his life in
bed. Others say he was operated on many times. Freddie's mother
had nursed him very carefully and lovingly all through his childhood.

When I first met Freddie this summer, I could tell that he was
not a well person. He was not strong enough to do any kind of
painting, plumbing, or construction work. He didn't have much
schooling on account of his ill health and therefore could not get a
job as a clerk in a store either. When I first met Freddie, I wondered what a man like that could do in life. How did he pass his
time? As I got to know him, I found out what Freddie did with his
time.

Have you really ever stopped to look at all the hundreds of little
children who hang around most everywhere in town — children
with nothing to do but throw rocks and play in the street, little
children with bare backs and no toys. And then, have you taken
a good look at the older boys who spend *their* time hanging around
the street corners, making remarks at everyone who goes by — older
boys who have nothing to talk about except how much they drank
last night and how much they drank the night before, older boys
headed for trouble with the law because they can get the excitement they want only by breaking the law. And then, have you
noticed the grown men in our town — men out of work, hanging
around much in the same way that the little children and the older
children do.

Freddie didn't work, didn't have any money, didn't have much

schooling, but let me tell you what he did with his time. He looked
at those little children with nothing to do, then he watched them
grow up; and you know, he saw that it was those same children who
became the boys on the street corners who make remarks to everyone who goes by. Freddie looked a little longer and realized that
those boys on the street corners became the men out of work, with
nothing to do.

Freddie didn't have much schooling; but he said, "Man, this is
wrong, those men without jobs never had a chance. Ever since
they were little children they have had nothing to do, nothing to
interest them, no one to give them some goal in life. The less they
have to do as children, the less they will have to do as adults."

Freddie was sickly, was not strong; but let me tell you what he
did. He gathered all the little children with their bare backs
around him and he told them stories; he told them about the
woods, and about little boys in school who did not study and about
little boys in school who did study. Then he got the little children interested in doing something, in making something of their
very own. He started them making model airplanes that would
really fly. Soon, around Freddie's neighborhood, there weren't so
many children playing on the streets and throwing rocks at each
other. They were forming clubs and making model airplanes and
listening to Freddie's stories.

Once the little children were organized, Freddie found that he
had some more hours in the day which he could use to work the
street corners, to work with the older boys who had nothing to do.
He asked them one day, "Have you ever heard of the Boy Scouts?"
Oh, the older boys thought that was very funny. Boy Scouts are
for kids, not for us men who hang out on the street corners. But
Freddie kept coming back to talk to these boys. He listened to
them laugh at him, just as they laughed at everyone who walked
by. Freddie didn't seem to mind. He kept coming back to talk
with these boys. One day, one of them asked him, "Mr. Freddie,"
he said, "how can I join the Boy Scouts?" In only a short time
Freddie had these same boys from the street corner formed into
well-organized scouts. He spent many hours with the boys, getting

them interested in the Scout program, giving them something to do that was good for the community and good for themselves as well. He had a bad heart, but he took these boys on long hikes and taught them how to cook out in the woods, how to act when a snake crawls in your tent. He told them about Moses and God and Jesus. Now these same boys weren't sneering at people who walked by; now they were helping old ladies across the street and trying to keep the streets clean; for a Boy Scout, he had told them, is helpful and also clean.

Once these older boys were organized, Freddie found that he had some more hours when he was free, not during the day but at night. He said that there must be other boys — and a lot of girls — in our town who had nothing to do and who would end up as adults with nothing to do. He began asking around about what these teen-agers did with their time. He found many who had nothing to do. With these, Freddie started what he called the Young American Citizens, a group which grew this summer to sixty members. These young Americans would meet together and talk about what they could do for their country. Their motto was: "Ask not what your country can do for you; ask what you can do for your country." They talked about voting; they talked about the war in Vietnam and what they could send to our boys over there. They talked about what a great country they had to live in and how they must be good citizens.

Now all of Freddie's time was taken up, mornings, afternoons, and nights. And Freddie was a sickly man who could never hold a job. He worked as hard as anyone I know.

On July 26th, when I arrived at St. Paul's Mission Center, I was met by some shocking news. Freddie had passed away at five that morning. I went by to see his mother a little later in the day and she said that Freddie's heart had just given out. She had taken him to the hospital, and they had given him some oxygen; but it was too late. When I left, I said to Freddie's mother, "Your son was a good man, one of the best I've met." "Yes," she said to me, "Freddie had the will, but he had no way."

What shall we say of a man like Freddie? A man who spent

half his life in bed, a man who died at the age of twenty-six, and yet a man who saw what was really going on in our town and *did* something about it. What shall we say about such a man? He knew that many adult Negroes had nothing to do and nothing to interest them because as children they had been allowed to roam the streets and sit idle all day on street curbs. What shall we say of a man who gave his whole life trying to get young Negro children interested in doing something for their community and for themselves as well? What shall we say of a sickly, uneducated man who had so little and did so much? A man who had the will but had no way.

I'll tell you what Jesus said about him, "This poor man has given more to his community than all the rich, given more than those rich white people who live downtown and put a lot of money in the collection plate on Sunday, given more than most — if not all — of you. You may not be rich, but you have more than Freddie. The rich people contribute out of their abundance, their wealth, but Freddie gave everything he had, his whole living. He gave — his life."

God bless you, Mr. Freddie. Help us, O Lord, to follow in the way that thy humble servant has set before us. Amen.

August 14. I'm back from church. It helps a preacher to know how the congregation is responding to his service, particularly his sermon. Are they listening? Or, are they merely focusing their eyes on you, thinking about the roast in the oven at home or the damn fool boss at the office?

Today, at Father Andrews's church, I was in a preacher's paradise. If the people were with me, they would nod their heads way up and way down. If they didn't understand or approve of what I was saying and doing, they would sit upright on the pew benches and look at me with puzzled eyes. They must have liked the sermon on Freddie for after it was over, they stood up, and before I knew what was happening, sang,

"Praise God from whom all blessings flow." They did not like my reading through the regular hymns because of the organist's absence. Next Sunday, the old lady who was so friendly to us before, the one with a name as old as Charleston, has agreed to lead the singing.

These Negroes this morning and most of the ones I've met this summer are so straightforward; by nature so open about everything. If they feel sadness, they scream in pain. If they feel joy, they stand up and sing about it. If they agree with you, they nod way up and way down. If they get mad at you, they get drunk and insult you or they break into your place and steal. If they love life, they dance accordingly. Now I know that, often, they play games with the white man, with me, pretending to like when they hate, pretending to be stupid when they aren't; but that's a game, not part of their nature. While society has deprived them of self-respect, has thwarted their growth, it has not superimposed on them the false and phony nature that middle-class white America is suffering from today, a nature which suppresses sadness, joy, truth, anger, love.

I was, through Freddie, trying to preach community responsibility to these Negroes — they need that. From their pews, they preached honesty and openness to me — I need that.

August 15. When I arrived at the center this morning, Adam, Michael, Mitchell, and Kinloch were all busy cleaning up. They spoke to me as pleasantly as ever, as though nothing had happened. When Adam was finally brought into the argument last Friday, he told Sally that he just had to "blow off a little every now and then." He didn't say why. Sally and I, in a telephone conversation, guessed that it was because he makes only $35 for a fifty-hour week. If a revolution is to arise in the Negro ghetto, I doubt if it will be led by fellows like these who "blow off a little" but never very much. No mention was made of the incident Friday.

I justify my shrugging off the events of last Friday by telling myself that I am being consistent with my overall approach of listening, of trying to understand.

It is very important that the white man appreciate the Negro's need, the *reasons* that cause him to blow off steam; but understanding alone will stunt his growth. The ghetto Negro must have someone to look him straight in the eye, and say, man to man, "All right, I'm going to see to it that you are paid a fair wage; I expect from you a fair amount of work in return." In their matriarchal culture, there has been no one to provide the image of the stern but just father who demands respect and responsibility, but who, at the same time, evokes self-respect and pride in his children. I have learned from Michael and Adam this summer, but I don't think I've given them much in return. Sally did!

August 16. By staying in this nice, cool office I've avoided the stampede and the noise of the children outside. The life of the ghetto, however, still finds its way to me — through the glass window and through such people as the woman who came in this morning with eviction notice in hand. Her rent was only $17 and she already had five dollars, but there was no way I could help her. My discretionary fund has given out and I have no money of my own. Besides that, if word gets out that we're buying off all eviction notices, we'll have everyone with rent problems from miles around coming in to see us. When I told her that we couldn't help, the woman squeezed her young daughter's hand, bowed her head, and cried softly. But I stood firm! Like the lady at the Welfare Department, I find myself getting tough, saving some, refusing others.

The problem that is taking up most of my time is one that Mrs. Martin brought to me. The city is building an auditorium on the street where she lives and is forcing her to sell her house to them. Since her husband died a few years ago and left no will, Mrs. Martin must find a way to have the pre-empted house put in her name. Her main problem though, is buying another house at a fair price and a price that she can afford. She asked me to help. I had planned to read a book of Tillich's sermons today, but how could I refuse to help Mrs. Martin, kind, gentle Mrs. Martin, the one who keeps Black-y-mo in shoes (or in "tennis," as she calls them).

First, she took me to the house that the city is going to appropriate, the house she and her husband spent most of their lives in. The city is paying her about $5,000 for it, a generous amount for such a place.

Then we went down to see the real-estate dealer Mrs. Martin has been talking with. He is trying to sell her a $7,000 house and says he's going to try to find a savings and loan company that will finance the $2,000 difference. In spite of the fact that the realtor called fifty-four-year-old Mrs. Martin, "Elizabeth," he was most cordial and answered all her questions clearly and in detail. It sounded as though she was all set.

But then Mrs. Martin took me to see the house she wants to buy. Now, I'll admit that I know very little about real estate, but I do know that house isn't worth any $7,000. In the first place, it's in poor repair on the outside. In the second, it's only a few feet away from what will soon be a major highway.

I am reasonably certain that the real-estate man would have

offered the house to a white person at the same price. The trouble comes in because Mrs. Martin has no idea of how to bargain and argue with a white businessman. She does not know that you never accept the first offer but that you make a counter offer instead so that, hopefully, you can settle at some price in between. When I was making installment loans in the bank, I remember how Negroes would always buy their automobiles at the highest price, then come to us and pay, without question, whatever interest we demanded. (Fortunately, our rates were all much the same.) What kind of match is Mrs. Martin for a good salesman!

Before she had asked me to help, she had practically committed herself to the offering price. I phoned the dealer and told him that I thought the price entirely too high; but he was unimpressed with my arguments.

Since I'm leaving in a few days and will not be able to help her shop around, I really don't know how to advise Mrs. Martin. She has got to buy something fast, within the next two months. "There aren't many houses for sale to colored," she tells me. And the next dealer may not only be a "good salesman," but a crooked one as well. Charleston has its fair share of those criminals who make their living on the ignorance and the helplessness of others. I'm told that they do this sort of thing: First, they talk a person like Mrs. Martin into putting up $5,000 toward a $9,000 home. Then they lend him or her the balance at 10 percent interest. And then, finally, when the mortgagee cannot possibly make the payments, they foreclose, sell the house to a secret partner for $6,000 and leave Mrs. Martin, or whoever it happens to be, practically penniless, with no home at all. So, do I advise Mrs. Martin to pay more than she should to the "good" salesman? Or, do I advise her to wait and shop some more, hoping that some crook will not grab hold of her?

This afternoon, Josh arrived about an hour before the boys' meeting was scheduled. Today, for the first time, he wore a "Freedom Now" button, which was attached to his belt. I invited him to come into the office to cool off, and soon we found ourselves talking in a free and friendly sort of way. While Josh was telling me about his past life, I was thinking that he reminds me of someone I once knew; but I can't figure out who it is.

He *is* the son of the lady who organized the Harlem political campaign and of the man who's a major in the army — but only by adoption. He is the real son of an alcoholic woman, whom he didn't meet until he was thirteen and who is now in a mental institution, and of an unknown man. Josh spent his childhood in blackest Harlem being moved from one foster home to another. At the age of thirteen he was so unhappy with one family he was sent to that he ran away and set out on his own, working at a supermarket. A few months later, he was arrested by the police and sent to some correctional home for juvenile delinquents. While there, he hit a guy over the head with a bottle and was summarily sent to the "pit" for a week of solitary confinement.

On being released from reform school, Josh was turned over to more foster parents who this time let him go his own way. Now he did what he wanted, slept wherever he felt like sleeping. But during this period, his junior and senior years in high school, he studied diligently for the first time and made all A's. When his stepmother met him three years ago, he was walking in a picket line. It was late and cold and he was one of the last three or four there. "Why don't you go home and get some warm food in you," she said, "You've done enough work for today." After a few embarrassing hems and haws, Josh told this lady who was to become his mother that he had no home to go to for supper. She took him home with her, and there he stayed.

"Josh," I said, at one point in the conversation, "tell me something. You're obviously a pretty sharp guy. Did you develop all that spit and polish in the last three years?"

"Oh no, I started looking out for myself long before that."

"Well how'd you break out of what seems to be dead-end, the apathy, the uh, uh, the, you-know-what-I-mean, of the ghetto?"

"Yeah, I know what you mean; but I really can't say. Maybe, it was when the judge, that white bastard, put me in the reform school. Or, maybe it was when I had to spend that time in solitary. One day, I realized that I was going to have to make my own way. I had had all the shit from them I could take."

"I admire your guts, fellow, but let me ask you something else. I always thought guys like yourself who break out of the ghetto tried to stay as far away from it as possible. How come you're working here in this place?"

"Man, I got out of the ghetto so I wouldn't have to take all the horse manure those people take. I didn't get out so I could run from my people. Those boys outside there right now, that's my home, the only home I've ever really had. That is except for my brother."

"Your brother?"

"Not really my brother, but since neither one of us had a brother, we looked on each other that way. Say, you know, he's an officer in the Navy now."

"That's fine. How'd you get close to him?"

"I first met him at one of the foster homes. He was older than me, but he took an interest in me and told me that along with being a wise guy, I was a smart kid and should do something with myself. I'd laugh at him. I even hid his glasses when he was trying to study. But then, maybe it was in the pit, I began to wish I had stayed at that foster home and studied as hard as he had. When I got the chance, I did."

"What are you going to do when Uncle gets through with you?"

"Shit, man, I've got it all planned. I'm going to begin work on my college degree this fall, taking an extension course at the base, and then when I get that, I'm going to law school. You see (he thumped his "Freedom Now" button) I'm going to beat the world at its own game. But it's boys like those guys out there who keep me going."

"Speaking of 'freedom now,' Josh, have you had any trouble in Charleston so far?"

"No, but I've stayed on the base for the most part."

"Well, what about the downtown theaters? Anyone give you any trouble there?"

"Listen, baby" — he was grinning — "if they give *me* any trouble, there's going to be some busted asses around."

"You're quite a guy, Josh."

August 17. This morning, when I arrived at the center, I walked straight up to Mrs. Martin and told her that I'd been sleeping on it and I thought she ought to offer the realtor $1,500 less than his asking price. She said she would take my advice.

If the realtor doesn't accept this offer — and he probably won't, at least, for the moment — Mrs. Martin will be doing the right thing. Even if she ends up making a deal with a conman after I leave, she will be doing the right thing. I've learned this summer that oftentimes you must act to do what is right *now*, regardless of future consequences. I've learned this in a small way from Mrs. Martin herself. I'll never forget that day she pulled out those two soiled bills to give to Black-y-mo. Mrs. Martin didn't stop to worry about the future, about the fact that her own family needed the money; she saw a need and she acted at once to meet it. "Freedom now" for Josh is punching an insulting white man in the face; "freedom now" for Mrs. Martin is refusing to pay more for a house than it's worth.

She must assert herself at all costs. But oh — what a painful thing for Mrs. Martin to do! She came into my office to telephone the realtor and asked me to get on the other line to help her out. I refused. This is her job. When she began to talk on the phone, I pretended to be busy at my desk. She wouldn't tell the realtor, at first, why she was calling. Instead, she hemmed and hawed and talked about the loan and the insurance. Finally, trying to sound unemotional, she told him that $5,500 was the best she could offer.

I don't know what the real-estate man said in response. I do know that a tear rolled down Mrs. Martin's brown cheek. She was nodding her head up and down as though the man was in the room. "Yes sir, yes sir, yes sir, yes, yes sir," she was saying. I wrote out a note in large letters for her to read. "Don't worry. He's only talking business. $5,500, no more." When she hung up, I did not ask her any questions. Instead, I went over to her and put my hand on her shoulder and reminded her of what she once told me. "Remember, Mrs. Martin," I said, "the Lord makes the back to bear the burden."

Sending his children to an integrated camp is the burden of the Southern white; haggling with a businessman over real property is the burden of the Southern Negro. Mrs. Martin must get rid of her feeling that the white realtor, the white banker, the white lawyer, or — for God's sake — the white mission center worker is doing her a favor by dealing with her at all. She gives money to the others; she gives insight and beauty to me.

August 18. No entry.

August 19. I do hope I have some peace and quiet in the office today. I have several things to write about. I must begin with the party night before last.

Most of the boys from the crowd I grew up in were there. They have all done well for themselves — doctors, lawyers, bank officers. All are good husbands and good fathers. Twenty years from now, they will be the leaders in Charleston. While we were growning up, these young men knew pretty well what they wanted in life. The doctors have thought all along that they would be doctors. The lawyers have thought all along that they would be lawyers. Since I changed my mind so many times, they called me "Indian Chief."

Doctor — lawyer — Indian Chief
Doctor — lawyer — Episcopal Priest

There's a section in my night world called Rainbow Row. The houses, built touching each other, are painted yellow, green, blue, tan, and pink. Most of them have wrought-iron balconies in front and courtyards in back. The party wasn't held in one of the famous Rainbow Row houses, but it was held in a house very much like those. My wife describes the interior of the house as "lovely." The living room is the perfect balance between antiquity and comfort. My friend, the host, is indeed prosperous and not yet thirty.

History repeats itself. When our gang first emerged from the lawless multitude of dirty-cheeked boys in short pants who roam our section of town — emerged and solidified — we isolated ourselves from girls. Those were the days of the Boy Scouts and the Sunday School plots. Those were my days. I was popular, maybe even a leader.

Then the girls began moving in on us. First, there were games of kick-the-can, then hot dog roasts, then impromptu dances every Saturday night. Somehow, in the new order of things, I lost my self-confidence. It was partly my fault. I once picked a fight with a fellow smaller than I in front of the girls — then backed down and ran. It was partly the crowd's fault. When one of the boys bought a Model A Ford, he'd often take three of us for rides, himself and the two others in front, me in the rumble seat. And it was partly the fault of fate. About that time, Al Capp came out with that awful character named Barnsmell. And dammit all, Barnsmell and Barnwell are the devil's first cousins. So, first I was Barnsmell, then Smell. By the time I was a senior in prep school, I was Smelly, that is, in Charleston. At the prep school itself, I was called Bill, Will, Willie, seldom William, my name.

Then we went to college, got married, and began our professional careers. Gradually, my self-confidence began coming back to me, but more *outside* than *in* Charleston. My first attempt at seminary was probably in some sense a flight from the crowd. But now I'm at seminary because I like it. There's Boy Scout work and there's Sunday School plots.

At the party night before last, I felt as sure of myself as I did that day when I led the campaign to impeach, if not assassinate, our sixth grade Sunday School teacher. Talking with two friends, a doctor and a businessman, I stated my positions on race with so much conviction that I threatened even myself. They listened to me. I mean, they really listened. It's a good feeling to be listened to. Moreover, one of them volunteered to help us at the center in any way that he could. I told him that he would be working with Negroes from Harlem who wear "Freedom Now" buttons; but he said that was all right, that he was damn sick and tired of no one trying to help the Negroes in Charleston. "If I can only help one person. Even if it prevents me from ever going into politics — and it may — I'll do what I can."

My story continues with the events of yesterday afternoon and last night. True to his word, my old friend was at the center in time for the Boys Club meeting. He seemed quite impressed with the discipline and the interest of the boys. "It really means something to them, doesn't it," he said. My friend asked if he could speak with the boys about scouting. This he did, and with a great deal of ability. The boys liked and respected him. Then he sat down and talked with Josh and Paul about camping areas and available transportation and about how he might help in the future. Josh agreed to make up a list of the equipment the troop would need. Before my friend left for the day, I took him by to see the Gray family, where he met Black-y-mo and the other children and sat down and talked at length with Mrs. Gray about what he might do professionally to help. He made no comment to me on the way out.

Last night was the night of the city-wide Boy Scout meeting. My friend had to leave, but Josh, Paul, and I decided to go out for a hamburger before we went to the meeting. As I climbed into the car, I was faced with this question: Should I drive toward a white or a Negro restaurant? To avoid making the decision myself, I asked Josh stupidly, "Do you know any good eating places around here?"

"No," said he, "the only restaurants I know are down on Wentworth Street." He was clearly referring to white restaurants, some of the "nicest" in town. I thought about people I might see at those places, and me in the company of Negroes, and I muttered something about the fact that they might be too far, and I drove away in the opposite direction. The first place we came to was a Negro combination barroom and hamburger joint.

Inside, there were two high school girls standing at the carry-out counter. Nice-looking girls, just standing there. So, while I was ordering the hamburgers, Josh was asking them for their telephone numbers. His passes at them were subtle at first, then obvious, and finally, downright obnoxious. The Negro waitress scowled. She had seen Josh's kind before, or so she thought. One of the high school girls was giggling, the other seemed scared. By the time our food was ready, Josh had his arms around both of them and was holding them tightly. Paul, who, as usual, had been quiet, almost had to drag Josh out of the place when we were ready to leave. On the way out, Josh pinched a third girl, right on the rump.

We drove to the city-wide Boy Scout meeting in silence. Had I once again hurt Josh? By not driving to a white restaurant, had I reminded him that he and I live in two different worlds? Had I driven him to the mood of the loneliness of the pit? That mood in which he realizes that he has too much self-respect and ambition to be at home in the Negro world of his past — the world of greasy, slummy hamburger joints — that mood in which he realizes that, because his skin is brown, he cannot live in the white man's world either. What do you do when you are that lonely? When the darkness begins to engulf you, leaving you by yourself in confusion and pain, what do you do? I get sick at my stomach; and if I'm lucky, some kid comes along wanting to play horseshoes. Josh gets sick too; and it he's lucky, some high school girls come along wanting to play barroom games with him.

Though Josh was depressed, he didn't let it interfere with his job. He, in effect, got out of bed and reported to work as usual. His job is to organize those boys, to give them the chance that he didn't have when he was their age. So, at the meeting, he went right to work: asking the other scoutmasters questions, taking notes on what the speaker said, making suggestions from the floor that everyone listened to. He even put me to work trying to locate some Negro Boy Scout advertisement posters to replace the lily-white "Join Us" signs we have on our bulletin board at the center.

I returned home from the meeting about ten. The white friend who is going to help Josh had been trying to get in touch with me and had left word for me to call him back, no matter what time it was. When I got him on the phone, he said that at about nine he had taken three large bags of groceries to the Grays and had found four of the children sleeping in their dirty clothes on the floor. Then he drove home to his air-conditioned, old-Charleston-brick house, and he thought about what must go on in Mrs. Gray's mind when she wakes up in the middle of the night, and he thought about his air-conditioning and his carved four-poster, and he knew he would not sleep that night.

"Barnwell," he said, "I've got three cots and mattresses and some sheets in the back of my car. How about going with me to take them to the Grays."

"Sure, I'll meet you tomorrow at ten."

"No, I mean let's go right now."

I've never visited any of those slum homes at night. I'm told that the place changes its complexion after eight. It could be dangerous. And I didn't much want to wake up the Grays. But then, I like my friend's determination to do the right thing now. "Okay, sure," I said, "come on over and get me."

We woke Mrs. Gray up when we arrived at the little house; but it didn't bother my friend. Rather than just pile the cots and mattresses at the doorway as I would have done, he walked right in, stepping over the children, and demanded that Mrs. Gray and I help him set up the cots and make the beds. In our amazement, Mrs. Gray and I both laughed out loud. Then this friend, who at one time wanted to be the governor, put his hand on his chin and said, "Let's see, we can put two on this one, three on this; I believe only one will fit on the little cot. That'll leave just the baby to sleep in bed with you, Mrs. Gray. You need sleep more than any of them."

The three of us lifted the children, still sleeping, onto the cots. One, two, three, four, five, six, seven. One, two, three, four, five, six, *seven*. Where'd the other one come from? I thought there were only six. Who knows! My friend and I said good night and left.

"You know, old man," I told him, "the best thing you did tonight wasn't bringing those beds. It was making them up and tucking the children in. I've learned something from you tonight." He smiled.

I was able to write the above entry because today was a quiet day in the office. Richard, as usual, was watching me from the other side of the window most of the day, his face squashed against the cool glass. We have in the office a stethoscope that some government doctor left here a few months ago. Everyone who comes into this office tries it out. It's been plugged into the ears of bug exterminators, Head Start directors, Wildcats, and Panthers. "Richard," I motioned to him "come on in here." And when he was in, "How'd you like to be Doctor Richard?" He nodded his head, he'd like that. I sat him down in the big swivel chair and fitted the strange-looking instrument in his ears. He gave me that big toothy smile of his when he heard his own heart beat. "Now, Richard," I said, "I want you to examine the children of St. Paul's one by one." He nodded his head, still smiling. By now, at least eight curious children were clustered at the window looking at us. I let them in one at a time. Each walked right up to the doctor for his examination; and Richard, amidst the applause of the rest of the children, did his job well.

I was surprised that he knew some of the doctors' words, which he would run together accenting only the first syllables. I was not surprised that he knew some four-letter words, all of which he accented. It went something like this: "PULLdonyoushirt, SHITman, HEARTsokay. NEXTchile."

After each child had seen the doctor twice and some three

times, Richard pulled the stethoscope out of his ears, got up, and — without a word — walked out of the door, either not hearing or ignoring my calls and the children's calls to come back. About ten minutes later when all the children were outside and I was back at the desk waiting for the rest of the afternoon to pass, Richard appeared once again at the window, watching me as before.

In the last three weeks, I've thought a lot about Richard. In fact, he hasn't given me much choice. You know, he's like the world — retarded! We can make ourselves laugh for a while, do better for a time, improve the conditions in the ghetto for a moment of history; but the old world just doesn't change much. Mrs. Martin, Josh, my friend, me, we're all doing better now; but soon, like the world, we'll forget about what we were doing — our courage, our work, our fellowship, our joy — and we'll go back to our old ways of staring blankly and unknowingly through the glass window.

August 20. I am fascinated by a comment that someone has made to me, that there may be a connection between the luster of old Charleston and my present idealism. I am fascinated by something else, my relationship to the invisible man Ralph Ellison describes in his great book. Something tells me that these two fascinations are basically connected, in fact inseparable. After all, the invisible man came from the South and he was an idealist too.

Today is Saturday and I'm going to sit here at the typewriter in the junk room until I come to some understanding on these matters. I should be taking my wife to the beach since I promised her I would. But I feel that I must sit here and work this thing out.

Some years ago, the hero of Ellison's book (let us simply call him Ellison) found that he was invisible. He discovered that, as a Negro, he was so unimportant in the eyes of the world that people saw right through him, missing him as a person. In the last ten or fifteen years, but this summer in particular, I have found that, as a member of old Charleston society, I am opaque, so tied up in myself that I block God's light from shining through me. This summer I've met many Negroes who are invisible in the sense that Ellison speaks of. But I've come to realize that these same people, while they are invisible to the world, are at the same time *transparent* to God's light, which shines clearly through them.

Also, in the last ten or fifteen years, but this summer in particular, I've found that while the people of old Charleston are opaque and block God's light, they are, nevertheless, fully developed persons in the sense that they have a strong identity and self-consciousness which has grown out of generations of living in this Southland, this city. They have body. They are a people. A kind of light does come from them; they are seen as persons; and that gives them luster, the luster of Rainbow Row, the luster of old churches and old-Charleston brick. But God's light does not shine through them as it does with those transparent Negroes.

Ellison hates himself because he is invisible; he longs for body, not the opaque body of old Charleston, but the body that matures and grows strong feeding on the bread of self-consciousness and identity — those things which give Charleston its luster. I hate myself because I am opaque; I long for transparency, not invisibility, but the kind of openness and purity of the Negroes I've gotten to know this summer. But Ellison and I, we're ambivalent. He also wants the

transparency of his grandfather, who was a slave and "invisible" but who made God visible for him. I also want my body,
my full manhood, my Charleston. I want people to call me
"William."

Now we're both idealists. He's a crushed one at the end of
the book, but one who vows to come out of his basement
room, which he has lit up artificially. I'm not crushed yet, but
since *I* also live in Richard's world, my days are probably num-
bered. As idealists, we both long for a perfect world in the
future; but our longing really comes from a longing for the
past, his for his enslaved grandfather and hot buttered yams,
mine for my Charleston and cold pickled shrimp. And now
that Ellison knows he is invisible, he cannot be entirely transparent. He has body. He stands erect. Now that I know I am
opaque, I cannot be fully body. I cannot block God's light
entirely. I am forced to lay down my life.

We're left dangling in Richard's world — he and I — longing for a perfect future, for the imperfect past, longing for
complete body, complete transparency.

Let me speak of my past. I guess I love Charleston as much
as anyone. Every time I come back home, cross one of the
bridges that connect the mainland with the peninsula, and
smell that pluff mud, I tingle all over. This is my home, a
colony of heaven, my land of milk and honey, the world God
created for me. I'd be living here right now, working at the
bank, maybe even living in Rainbow Row, if it hadn't been for
the fact that in those high school years, those years of riding in
the rumble seat, I was forced to try to find a home elsewhere, a
place where I could grow in my own way. At prep school in
North Carolina, under the influence of an English teacher, I
began to discover that the world was bigger than my city, my

crowd. In this discovery, a strange thing happened. I found that I was able to look at Charleston from within it — I was still a struggling member of the crowd — yet also from outside it. I've come to find out that, as a member of the crowd, I am opaque; I've found out that, as an exile from the crowd, I am forced to be transparent to God's light. But, in the words of the Welfare Department, I am also left "ego deficient." The Jews felt this deficiency when they were kicked out of Israel in their exile. Tillich felt this, if I read him right, when he was kicked out of Germany.

What happens now? For the Jews, says Tillich, the God of Abraham, the God of Isaac, and the God of Jacob *remains* their God! He is no longer bound to the land, no longer a god of success, no longer a national god; but he *is* their God. Tillich's God is not bound by Germany and German theology. My God is not bound by the crowd, by Charleston. But he's still our God. At the same time, we — the Jews, Tillich, I — are stripped of our protection, the identity upon which we relied ultimately. We are left with Ellison, in exile, left to roam, wondering who we are.

Now there is only us and God, nothing in between. In a sense, we are forced into the position that Jesus was in. In our exile, we are forced to lay down our life, our fatherland. There is, however, a fundamental difference between us and Jesus. In him, says Tillich, is the only true paradox; for in Christ, God's light and man's body exist together perfectly. Jesus was perfectly transparent, perfectly man. He did not live on bread alone, but he did live on bread. The rest of us are not paradoxical in the same way. We are mostly transparent, mostly body, or we dangle awkwardly in between. But Jesus was both; he was complete. He lives in paradox; we live in contradiction. To be me, fully me in the transparent sense, there can be no Charleston, nothing in between God and myself. To be me, fully me in the self-conscious sense, there can be only Charleston. Only as a member of the crowd can I be me, can I be "William."

This summer, my work in relation to the crowd is double-edged. I'm an enemy of the crowd, trying to destroy it so that God's light will break through. But I also work to gain respect from the crowd, a certain dignity. My working with "niggers" will make them say, "He's not dependent on us any more. Look at what that fellow is doing on his own. We didn't know old Smell had so much to him. And listen to him bellow out at us in such a deep voice about the injustices in our city. Wow!" Right now, I am moderately successful in destroying the crowd and in gaining respect from them. But what happens if I am completely successful, or if I completely fail? Will I, like Ellison, isolate what's left of me and seek refuge in some basement room?

Now let me speak of Ellison's past; for it is that, as an exile from the crowd, I have learned something about this summer. I've met his grandfather a number of times, in people who are invisible, who are usually missed entirely, but people who make God visible. They know neither of their invisibility nor of their transparency. I've met him in the person of Freddie, who allowed God's love of fellowman to shine through him in a near-perfect way; in Adam and Mrs. Martin, who let God's understanding shine through; in Rosa and Mrs. Gray, who let God's love of family shine through; and I've met him all at once in the many children and the people of the Big Dance, who let God's love of life shine clearly through. Them and God. Nothing in between. You see in them not good people by society's standards, not good works, if you measure good works by success, not strong ego, not body; but you do see God's light. People fed not by bread, but by every word that proceeds from the mouth of God. Not accomplishment — but life, childlike life, the life that a loving God gave to man. These people whom I've known are Ellison's land of milk and honey. When he found out that they were transparent, he found out at the same time that they were invisible; and he could not return to them completely.

You see, he found out that even though they make God visible, they make themselves fools, irresponsible, the bottom of society, "yes sir, yes sir" people, and they give birth to children who never have a chance. They are the idiot of Dostoevski, through whom light shines supremely, but who, at the end, is nothing. . . . Nothing! They approach being Christ figures in the sense of transparency; but — and this is a hard thing to say — they are the anti-Christ in the sense that they do not grow into maturity. For Christ is fully body, fully man. He is a king, he is responsible, he never says "yes" to any man unless he really means it. He gave the world a chance. These people are like John the Baptist, who prepared the way, who said in the Fourth Gospel that Jesus will increase while I decrease. Even unto the grave, and — God help me — even unto Freddie's grave; for Freddie was a fool. Let us preach about them, let us give them our highest praise; but let us not call them Christ. There is only one Christ.

Let us praise Charleston, let us love that pluff mud smell and those old, old houses; but — God help me — let us not rely upon it ultimately. There is only one Christ.

Ellison, you can't go home, you have no home. But then, neither do I. When, however, you look backward to your grandfather, you at once begin to look forward. Soon your land of milk and honey looms beautifully and ideally on the horizon in front, not behind. It's perfect now, fully God's and fully man's. Only we'll never reach the Promised Land — you and me. We'll dangle between the Christ of body and the Christ of transparency. We'll love both, we'll hate both; we can be neither. But — and this is our one consolation — we'll begin to understand both. "For now we see in a mirror dimly, but then face to face. Now I know in part; then I shall understand fully, even as I have been fully understood." And then that one consolation will be taken away and we too will stare blankly and unknowingly through the glass window.

My watch tells me that it's midnight; my wife tells me that it's time to go to bed, for tomorrow I have to get up and preach at Father Andrews's church.

VIII

When Night is Turned to Day

Crossing the Red Sea into the land of identity, crossing the River Jordan into the land of the exile is not easy. Man must die to himself to do it. And what man can die alone?

Watch out for Adam, good Lord, watch out for those white parents. Open your Red Sea waters for him, Lord. Stay there at their side in their exile. Deliver them, Lord. . . . Allow Adam's children and the white parents' children to sing of you as the prophetess Miriam sang of old:

> Sing to the Lord, for he has
>   triumphed gloriously;
> the horse and his rider he has
>   thrown into the sea.

Christ is the world's true light
Its Captain of salvation,
The Day-star clear and bright
Of every man and nation;
New life, new hope awakes,
Where'er men own his sway:
Freedom her bondage breaks,
And night is turned to day.

In Christ all races meet,
Their ancient feuds forgetting,
The whole round world complete,
From sunrise to its setting:
When Christ is throned as Lord,
Men shall forsake their fear,
To ploughshare beat the sword,
To pruning-hook the spear.

One Lord, in one great Name
Unite us all who own thee;
Cast out our pride and shame
That hinder to enthrone thee;
The world has waited long,
Has travailed long in pain;
To heal its ancient wrong,
Come, Prince of Peace, and reign. Amen.

— The Hymnal, 1940

AUGUST 21. Today, after church, I took my wife to the beach.

August 22. Several weeks ago, at a cocktail party, a certain lady I talked to about the conditions of the slums must have listened to me; for she, in turn, talked to one of her most conservative friends, Sarah, about these conditions in our city, and this friend came to the center today to talk with me about it. She is a schoolteacher and told me frankly that she had fought the integration of the schools, in her words, "tooth and nail." This year she will be teaching her first integrated class. But it was not to argue integration that she came to see me.

Sarah came to see me simply because she knows there are needs to be met in our city. "William, is there any way I can help?" she asked.

"Yes," I said without batting an eye, "we can use you in some way, I'm sure. What kind of things are you most interested in?" Some ghetto workers would not touch a person like this, would not have anything to do with a segregationist, particularly a vocal one. But I'm not built that way. In fact, I have entirely different ideas. When you put people together to work together, you often find that they begin thinking of each other as people and that great intellectual ideas and emotional prejudices are not so important. That's been true to some extent with Josh and me. I hope it proves to be true with this lady and the ghetto children.

She said that she wasn't much on club work but would be interested in tutoring. "I've just the job for you," I said eagerly. And then I told her about Ned, whose real name is Nat. Beginning about a month ago, this young fellow with a smile as big as Richard's and skin as dark as Black-y-mo's started coming to the center, not for a few hours at a time like most of the kids, but for all day. I give him the Boy Scout salute which he returns every time we pass each other, but other than that, I haven't gotten to know him very well. When Ned, who says he's eleven, joined the Boy Scout troop, Kinloch Manigault began taking a special interest in him. Right away, he realized that Ned couldn't read the simplest of words, not even the "on" and the "my" of the first line of the Scout oath, and Ned is eleven years old. Then Kinloch tried to find out where Ned lives and discovered that some of the time Ned lives with his grandmother, some of the time he lives with his mother, but most of the time he lives in between, which means that he sleeps on people's doorsteps, in the back-yard of the center, and in the alley behind Mr. Dick's store. He eats what anyone will give him and naturally he has gotten to know Mrs. Martin quite well.

"Now, Sarah," I continued, "Ned is at a turning point in his life. He's got some sense — in fact he may even be a bright boy — but if someone doesn't do something with him soon, he's going to start going downhill, and fast. Only this morning, he threw an empty whiskey bottle at one of the old colored women in this neighborhood. If you could take him for one afternoon a week and try to teach him how to read, you may make the difference in his life." Then I told her about the fact that Ned may or may not show up for the tutoring sessions but that was part of the whole cycle. She seemed to understand the depth of the problem and agreed to try to help.

Then we got hold of Ned, who looked tired and shabby but who, nevertheless, was smiling as usual. I introduced him to Sarah and said, "Ned, boy, see if you can read the Scout oath for this lady here." He looked down at the page and seemingly read through the first paragraph without any trouble. After my build-up to Sarah about Ned's lack of education, I confess to being embarrassed when he read so well. But then I covered up the last two paragraphs of the oath with my hand and Ned kept right on "reading." When he finished, he smiled proudly.

"Ned, you've done well to memorize that oath. Now this lady is going to teach you how to read it. And then, Josh will really be proud of you." Ned liked the idea. Sarah asked him some questions and seemed to be pleased at the prospect of tutoring him. I think she'll do a good job. Hell, she may even turn out to be like the second son that Jesus speaks of, who said he would not — but he did!

In my eagerness to accept Sarah as a tutor for Ned, I'm thinking, of course, of what it will do for him; but I'm also thinking of what it will do for Sarah. I don't mean in the way of making her feel sweet and good and self-sacrificing. I'm thinking about what will happen when Sarah really comes to know Ned, to see him, to believe in him. And I'm thinking about the day when Sarah meets Josh and Paul, and Father Andrews.

Josh, Sarah, and me, the political and social spectrum in

three persons, all drawn together for different reasons — and I'm not sure what they all are — to shape Ned up. I can't tell you why the three of us, so different in outlook, are drawn so closely together today. Frankly it doesn't make sense.

We are like the man blind from birth. And Jesus spat on the ground and made clay of the spittle and annointed the man's eyes with the clay. The man went away and washed his eyes and came back — seeing. Now the Pharisees questioned the man who was once blind about this man Jesus, but the man could not tell them who Jesus is, or what he is. "Whether he is a sinner, I do not know; one thing I do know, though I was blind now I see." Josh, Sarah and me. I can't tell you why we are drawn together. Frankly it doesn't make sense. We're, all of us, sinners. Ned, like our world, is practically beyond hope. I do know this, though. We are blind but we begin to see. And sight is what this relationship will give us, Josh and Sarah and Ned and me. And what a splendid gift that is.

August 23. I know now who reminded me of Josh. He was right there, all the time, right in front of me; I missed him — blindly. They are both invisible, both have gained body, both are idealists, one is crushed, one is not — not yet.

Josh and I have grown up in different fatherlands, he in the ghetto and later in the militant Negro movement, me in old Charleston and later in the responding white movement. I still have avoided the integrated parties, but I have admitted my prejudice and have resolved to do something about it. Josh still wears his "Freedom Now" button — in fact, today he was wearing it on his collar, not his belt — but he has also seen beyond the militant movement. He lets me be me; I let him be Josh. Today, I realized that we are much closer to-gether than we are apart.

A few days ago, we asked Josh to type up a list of what the Boy Scouts need in the way of camping equipment. He brought that list, which he had prepared very carefully, in today. At the bottom of the list was a paragraph about what the boys really need. I copied it:

> I believe that I can truthfully speak for the boys of —— Street and the surrounding area when I say that they would enjoy the fun of hiking and camping with one another . . . to build their own fires and cook their own food . . . stalking wild animals . . . sending secret messages from hilltop to hilltop across a lake . . . swimming, diving, pad-dling canoes . . . sitting around a glowing campfire sing-ing, laughing and listening while someone tells stories. This is life for a boy. But for these boys to do this — SOME ONE MUST CARE. We, the Scout leaders, know that you CARE. Now please show the boys that you CARE. Thank you.

This is life for a boy. Josh, Josh. You've done what can't be done. You've maintained your "freedom-now" ideals and you've accepted the charity of this paternalistic, white-sponsored mission. You've maintained your dignity as a man, you've sacrificed your dignity — for your boys.

And then at the end of the paragraph Josh had added this poem:

> My needs are your needs, old needs . . .
> of bread and of love, of work and peace,
> of room to grow, and time to think, and long years
>   to live —
>   — Walter Benton

Today would be the last time I'd see Josh. We head back to Virginia this weekend, and Josh would not be able to come to the center before then. There is so much I had wanted to talk to him about, how I was prejudiced, how I knew what he was going through, how I was going through the same thing, only in a different way. I wanted to know more about his background, his views on things, what he thought about me. I wanted to know all of the things from his past that drive him so furiously forward.

Somehow I wanted to talk about these things with him, somehow I didn't. In a way, they had all been said, not spoken, but said. I gave Josh the rest of the information I had about the troop, my Virginia address to look me up, then a handshake with a "good-bye, Josh, and thanks," all I could say. He grabbed my hand tightly; I could see him mash his lips together. "Good-bye," he said. "You know you will be missed around here." Maybe Josh knew about me and my two worlds too.

August 24. My splitting of Christ into transparency and body last Saturday was lacking in something. Today, I found out what that was. I think I described Christ and the predicament of man accurately; but the Biblical Christ didn't come into this world merely to be described. We cannot just say that God was in Christ; we must say, with St. Paul, that God was in Christ reconciling the world to Him. Christ came into the world to help man overcome his predicament. There is movement in Christ — from God to man and from man to God.

If there is one single theme that runs throughout the Old

and New Testaments, it is that of movement — out of Egypt into Canaan, out of Canaan into the exile, back to Canaan, out of Galilee into Jerusalem, out of Jerusalem into the Gentile world, out of this world into the next. And then there is the mythical-psychological movement — out of the Garden of Eden into the fallen world of man, fallen but nevertheless the land of the tree of knowledge, then out of this world and into the next.

We do live in a retarded world; we are in a predicament. But there is movement. There's the kind of movement I saw that day at the white camp. That was movement of people out of Canaan into the exile; for those parents were willing to give up some of their old-South identity so that God's light could break through them and shine upon their children.

Then, there's the kind of movement I saw yesterday when Josh wrote that letter asking for money from the white benefactors of the center, and the kind that I saw the day before when Sarah and Ned met. Today, I saw still another kind of movement, but one that involved just as much of a crossing over from one land into another, just as much of a death and rebirth. Because there is movement — though it be limited — there is hope, which is unlimited.

Friends, today — was a great day. It was the day Adam, of his own accord, quit the mission center to take a new job, quit and cut his umbilical cord, and became a man. I didn't know what he had done until this afternoon. When I did come to realize that he hadn't been at the center all day, I asked around to find out if anyone had seen him. Finally, Michael told me. "Adam quit. He got him a job down at the Office of Economic Opportunity."

"You mean he just walked out on us? After four years at the center, he just up and quit? And why didn't he tell me anything about it?" I was mad, but did not stay mad long.

When I got Adam's new employer on the phone, he told me that Adam had come to see them about a job yesterday. By chance, they had a position open right then, and they hired him immediately. They are going to train him as a book-keeper and then put him on their regular staff. His salary will jump from $35 to $65. If all goes well, he will be making $80 a week within a year. Now, Adam has the chance to gain self-respect, to put that energy that causes him to blow off to positive use, to become a father who evokes self-respect in his children.

Adam is moving from the purity, the innocence, the simple beauty of the Garden of Eden into the world of man, from the invisibility of the Jewish slaves in Egypt across the Red Sea waters into the land of identity. He will no doubt lose some of his great and unmuddled understanding of human nature in the process of becoming a typical American, of learning how to live under the law. But he will move.

He came by the center late in the afternoon to pick up his check. He didn't seem to want to talk to me, but I pulled him aside anyway. "Good for you, Adam," I said. "I'm one hundred percent behind you, Bo." I could tell that he was quite nervous about his new job; and he's got good cause to be. Working nine to five in an office with a coat and tie on will be a completely new experience for him, a new world.

It was only four years ago that he was persuaded by Father Andrews to leave that gang of hoodlums he had formed, only two years ago that he was talked into marrying the woman

who had already given birth to his child, only one year ago that
he momentarily went back to his old ways and was caught and
given a suspended sentence for robbing the mission center of
food and selling it on the outside. It was less than two weeks
ago that he blew off by taking Linda's car and getting himself
drunk. Adam's new job will be as difficult as the white parents' decision. It will be as painful and as demanding for him
to keep that position as it will be for those parents to send
their children back to camp next year.

Crossing the Red Sea into the land of identity, crossing the
River Jordan into the land of the exile is not easy. Man must
die to himself to do it. And what man can die alone?

Watch out for Adam, good Lord, watch out for those white
parents. Open your Red Sea waters for him, Lord. Stay there
at their side in their exile. Deliver them, Lord. With your
mighty hand and your outstretched arm, with great terror,
with signs and wonders, bring them into the new place and
give them a land, a land flowing with milk and honey. Allow
Adam's children and the white parents' children to sing of you
as the prophetess Miriam sang of old:

> Sing to the Lord, for he has
> triumphed gloriously;
> the horse and his rider he has
> thrown into the sea.

Reconcile us to you, Lord. Bestow upon the invisible, body.
Bestow upon the opaque, transparency. Not so that the black
become white and the white become black, but reconcile us to
you Lord, you who are at once black and white, to your son
who is at once God and man. Let us meet there in you. Stand

there, Lord, at the going down of the sun; and our hope will be in you.

And one other thing, Lord, give Ellison, Josh, and me the strength to climb out of the hole of artificial light, the darkness of the pit, give us the strength, good Lord, to get out of bed even during our worst days and report to work as usual.

Thank you, Lord, thank you, Jesus.

IX

The Last Day

Soon we would be on the road again . . . crossing the Cooper River, passing through the land
of my grandfather, then by the stands where
Negroes weave and sell baskets, driving up the
Carolina lowcountry — south to north — out of
the land of milk and honey, into the land of
the exile, away from the perfume of heaven,
into the smell of gasoline fumes. The swamps
would be dark. . . . I would be thinking, asking myself a thousand questions about such
things as inner and outer conflicts, was I
"saved?" what does it mean to be "saved" anyway? thinking of the past, dreaming of the future. Of camp next summer, of Adam next
week, of Josh and of me.

◖

MY LAST DAY. I spent the morning finishing up my last chores at the center. First, I cleaned up Father Andrews' office, which had become grimy from the steady flow of young visitors who came in to see me this last week. Then I wrote most of the people who are doing volunteer work with the children, eight of them now, five white and three Negro. In my letter to the white workers, I said that if they could stick with the jobs they had set out to do, teaching sewing, advising the Boy Scout troop, tutoring, assisting Mrs. Calvin with the Girls Club, they would prove in a minature way that a white Southerner can respond positively to the sickness of the ghetto without compromising his basic beliefs and without selling out his homeland. What I didn't tell them is that, when they really get to know and love those young people and begin to learn from them, they may find themselves putting the kids first, themselves and their homeland second. If that happens, their changed attitudes will be the result of their decisions, not mine. Nor will they be the decisions of some glib, South-hating person who marches with an integration sign sitting securely on his back. Their decisions, not mine. I merely thanked Josh, Paul, and Mrs. Calvin. What else could I say to them?

After finishing my letters, I walked over to see Mrs. Gray in order to give her the names of two lawyers who had offered to help her try to locate her legal husband for support. When I arrived at her place, she told me that she had received her letter from the Welfare Department in the morning's mail. It was a form letter saying something about not being able to establish proof. There was a hand-typed sentence at the bottom which read: "According to our rules, your children are not deprived of parental support. We hope you have been able to work out satisfactory plans for your family." I can't say I was surprised. Our society does not think of the very bottom, the one lost sheep; it is too practical for that. Let's watch over the ninety and nine, and to hell with Mrs. Gray.

Someone else will have to respond sensitively and positively to Mrs. Gray's situation now. I've done all I can do. She'll probably go back to work and leave her nine-year-old and Blacky-mo at home to mind the little ones. After a while, a truant officer will stop by and demand that these two children go back to school. She'll say it's impossible; he'll say, "But the law's the law." Then they'll go down to the Welfare Department and run into another law, and the whole thing will begin all over again. Or, one of the six children will become seriously ill, and she'll have to quit work to nurse him. Then she'll come to the center for help. Maybe some young seminarian will be there and will go over with her to see the sick kid. He'll be shocked and will start raising hell with everyone in town who will listen to him, blaming them, blaming himself. The child either will die, like the one last March, or live; but either way, Mrs. Gray will go back to work and do the best she can for the remaining children. And life will go on. Society can't stop that, that's the one thing Mrs. Gray has got.

Just before I left, Father Andrews called. More bad news! He had returned from New England last night and had already heard about Adam's resignation. "Isn't that great," I said.

"Well, William," he replied, "what you apparently don't realize is that Adam has left his work at the center to take government jobs before. He'll be back here within a week looking for his old job back."

"I didn't realize that," I said. I didn't realize that.

When I get attached to a job — whether it has been successful or not — I don't like to hang around right before leaving. You never know what to say to anyone. So after I finished my chores this morning, I left and didn't return until late afternoon. But I kept busy in the meantime.

First, I took the five boys who had gone to camp down to the clinic to get additional shots, something I had promised the clinic I would do. They were all looking forward to school, enjoying the Scout troop, and planning how they could save up some money to go to camp on next year.

Then I went home to pack and prepare for the long trip tomorrow. My mother and father told me how much they would miss me. I wish I had a way to tell them how much I will miss them. I went upstairs and began packing. The room I had cleared of junk at the beginning of the summer was now full of junk again, my junk. Notes for this diary were scattered all over the place. I put up what I wanted to save and threw the rest away. I came across one page on which I had written, at different times, during the summer, conclusions to the diary. The first was written early when I was so shaken by the stinking ghetto conditions; the second was written after I was humbled by those white parents at camp; the third, only a couple of weeks ago. The three follow in the order they were written:

> And lastly, I've figured out the resurrection after my work this summer. If you want to keep on living after you die and continue to serve humanity, get yourself buried by one of those churches that was originally built in a fashionable neighborhood but one which has since turned into a slum. If you are lucky, the church will be converted into a community center; and over the years thousands of children will play on your tomb—everything from cops and robbers to follow-the-leader. They may even try to raise you while they dance around your grave. And the children won't hold your white skin against you.

And then the second entry:

> I wrote the above earlier in the summer. As the last entry in the diary I was going to tell what I did, tell what I learned and make the above statement in closing. But I'll tell you what. That statement stinks! It's cute, it's flip, but worst of all it's glib. After my work this summer, my final advice to myself and to anyone who may read this is: Don't be glib! If you are a segregationist, don't brush off the agonies of the ghetto by saying that you'll just send the maid home in a taxi. If you are an integrationist, don't just talk and preach and smugly carry signs and write books from a distance. But suffer, get involved personally and suffer. Only then will we approach the truth. GODDAMMIT, bleed! Only then will God bestow his saving grace upon our troubled land.

And then the last entry after my wife told me that the

above was too preachy — "if you don't have them now, you never will":

> All summer I have been debating with myself about how I would conclude my diary. Each time, my conclusion was quite different from the time before. The truth of the matter is, I am not ready to make any conclusions. My life's work has just started. Anyone who reads this can write his own conclusion. Or better still, he can get to know the people of the ghetto and write his own diary.

While I read this last entry, I thought to myself, what will my life's work be? I had asked the diocese to send me to St. Paul's next June when I finish seminary to be attached on a permanent basis. The diocese refused. "No," they said, "we're sending you to a small church in the country or in a small town. There you can learn what the parish ministry is all about." I got mad at the diocese at first, but now that I think about it, I believe they are right. If I am true to my own ideas about the necessity of developing a church consciousness, I must begin my ministry in a typical church setting, a place where people worship and meet together regularly, where they study their book. And besides that, I've never lived in the country.

Some day, maybe not too long from now, maybe a long time from now, I hope to return to the ghetto, even if it means giving up my church consciousness. But who can say what tomorrow will bring, what my life's work will be.

There you go again, Barnwell, dreaming, you've got to get that car packed. So I did. Just before leaving the house, I called the bank to get my bank balance since I hadn't bothered to keep up with it this summer. An old acquaintance, who, like the man at the club, has had his craw full of niggers, answered the phone. We chatted for a couple of minutes. Then he asked me what I was doing this summer. When I told him, he said, "You aren't becoming one of those kind, are you, William?"

"What do you mean?" I was stalling, hoping to put the battle off as long as possible.

"You know what I mean. Are you still a Charleston boy or are you an all-around sort of person?"

I swallowed hard, paused for what seemed to be an embarrassing length of time, then answered, "You're asking for a black or white answer. I'll give you a black one, I'm an all-around sort of person."

"Oh man, don't tell me that." There was genuine sadness in his voice. He left the phone and got my balance; and on returning, "It's $56."

"Minus or plus?" I asked. I can't tell you why, but suddenly I felt like kidding him.

Then he kidded me. "I don't know about that. All I know is that there's one of those OD overdraft marks by it. You worked in the bank, what does that mean?"

Still laughing to myself, I got in the car and drove up to the center for the last time. It was about four-thirty; the place was empty, except for Mrs. Martin, Linda, Michael, and Kinloch. They had run all the children out so that the floor could be mopped. First, I shook hands with Mrs. Martin and wished her good luck on her house. She told me that her sister in New York was glad I had talked her into waiting. Then, with Linda. We agreed that neither one of us knew what to say. I didn't realize, until our hands touched, how close we had become. Then, with Kinloch. I told him I was recommending him for Adam's position and that he had done a good job this summer. Then, with Michael. He and I have not spoken to each other much since the day Sally left. But I have noticed that he has been working harder than ever. He'll be going back to high school this year to finish up. "Michael," I said, "I know you are loyal to the center." He smiled warmly. I could not help but feel some guilt at how much easier I was getting off than Sally.

On the way out, I took down the lily-white Boy Scout "Joins Us" signs and put up that fan with the Negro Boy and Girl Scouts standing in front of an American flag, the one I had taken from Freddie's funeral. "One nation indivisible," it said. And then I went outside.

Soon we would be on the road again, tooting the boul for the last time, crossing the Cooper River, passing through the land of my grandfather, then by the stands where Negroes weave and sell baskets, driving up the Carolina lowcountry — south to north — out of the land of milk and honey, into the land of exile, away from the perfume of heaven, into the smell of gasoline fumes. The swamps would be dark, the water stagnant. My wife would be sleeping; I would be thinking, asking myself a thousand questions about such things as inner and outer conflicts, was I "saved"? what does it mean to be "saved" anyway? thinking of the past, dreaming of the future. Of camp next summer, of Adam next week, of Josh and of me.

Outside, a number of children were playing in my car, as they usually do in the late afternoon — turning the steering wheel, poking the lighter in and out, seeing who could roll the windows up and down the fastest. Andrew, who had been my cross-bearer, was there. Timothy, who pulled me through a rough day, was there. The boys that I had spent most of my time with this summer, the five who went to camp and Sneed and Goodie, were not there. Neither was Ned. Richard was sitting on the sidewalk, watching. As I walked out of the graveyard, up to the car, Black-y-mo, hiding in the bushes, jumped at me roaring like a lion and grabbed my hand with both of his. Then he climbed up my arm so that he could swing back and forth without touching the ground. "Can we go wit' you, can we go wit' you," they all chanted as they always do. Sometimes I take them when I drive around town on errands. But not today. "No, boys, I'm leaving this time for good. I won't be back." Climbing into the car, I thought to myself that there's something infinitely sad in that statement. But it was in my mind, not theirs. "Oh please, Mr. Barnwell, let us go wit' you, please, please." But I had gotten them all out now and was starting the engine. Black-y-mo was waving and laughing and fighting off the rest of the kids. Richard, whom we call "Doctor" now, was still sitting on the sidewalk, watching. I believe he smiled a little. When I pulled away from the curb, I did not look back.

Afterword

OCTOBER 12, 2009, was the day I turned seventy-one, but, infinitely more important, it was the day when St. John's Mission was consecrated as a new church in my hometown of Charleston, South Carolina. St. John's is the same place, that long-ago summer, I had my turnaround experience working under Father Grant and kept a journal that became *In Richard's World*. Then it was a kind of beat-up mission, a community center; now it is an official, elegant Episcopal chapel, rebuilt to serve the same neighborhood, still almost completely African American. The pastor and main inspiration behind the new St. John's, Father Dallas Wilson, known everywhere as Brother Dallas, called to invite me to attend the consecration and to speak briefly. I dropped what I was doing and flew up for the ceremony.

In the churches I have served in Boston and Washington, even at Trinity, New Orleans, preachers and speakers often talk easily about race and racism. But never do I remember a service so fully integrated across race, class, and age lines, a service so lively, so hopeful that our God through Christ will bring love and peace to the world. In St. John's case, this would be to the surrounding neighborhood, still poverty-stricken but not so much in need as it was in the 1960s.

Al Zadig, the rector of St. Michael's in Old Charleston, a church as white as its distinguished nineteenth-century steeple, gave a stirring sermon. Along with his congregation, Al was a key player in rebuilding and expanding St. John's. The mission center had come to an end about the time Father Grant died in 1985, then fell into

Originally published in William Barnwell's *Lead Me On, Let Me Stand*.

near ruin in the years that followed. An old friend, Al is a leader in bringing the races together in Charleston.

Several years ago Al and I set off in different directions in regard to issues related to gay and straight people. Like the new Episcopal bishop of the Diocese of South Carolina and so many of the clergy and lay members in that diocese, Al believes that openly gay men and women should not be considered for ordination to the priesthood and should not have their unions blessed, should not marry in our church. As I write my memoir, *Lead Me On, Let Me Stand*, many from his diocese are seriously considering withdrawing over these issues from what I call the National Episcopal Church. In their view, it is people like me who have withdrawn from the true church, those of us who have promoted gay unions, gay marriages, and now openly gay priests and bishops.

It would be great if we could all say, as Sam Lloyd of the Washington National Cathedral suggested years ago: *"There* we walk," instead of "Here I stand—and I ain't moving." But on issues of sexuality, there seems little room for negotiation. We can, however, find much common ground in our work to bring the races together and to build a more economically just world. Maybe that will be an important step toward reunion one of these days or centuries when the old hostile elements come together once again.

Built in 1837 on what was a graveyard, St. John's had been a thriving church before it eventually became the mission center where I worked. There are still full-length graves in the side yard of the new church. When I was working there in 1966, the preteens used to play follow-the-leader across those same graves just as my friends and I had done in the St. Philip's churchyard when we were that age. Al's sermon had nothing to do with sexual orientation. He held up a stone from the yard outside as though it were a bone from one of the ancient graves and said, referring to Ezekiel, "Those old bones on which St. John's was built in 1837 will rise again. God will give new life and flesh to the old bones. And through St. John's and through the Holy Spirit, God will bring new life and hope to this part of Charleston."

Just about all those who gave the various speeches were white. I wish whoever had planned the service had given Brother Dallas, an African American, a more prominent part. He just introduced people, few of whom wanted to talk about race, racism, or integration. And yet this lovely congregation, looking as much like Old *and New* Charleston as I could imagine, was *doing* integration, even though they couldn't talk about it. The much-admired mayor of the city, Joe Riley, gave a powerful blessing to the congregation. "St. John's," he said, "will give new meaning to the word *brotherhood* in our beloved city."

In my talk, I told of how, forty-three years before, Goodie, from our St. John's Boys Club, had advertised a community dance with posters that read, "Hi Batmen, hi Robins. Come some, come all, to the Big Dance, eight o'clock till the Pot o' Honey." "The Big Dance," I said, "held right where you are sitting in this church sanctuary, was a life-changing experience for me. I saw up close how even in the squalor, the depravity, the injustice of a terrible slum, how people could claim a life full of love and meaning. Later, the night of the Big Dance, I wrote in my journal, 'Dance, man, dance. Live, man, live.'"

I then told of how Father Grant, my mentor as well as my supervisor, was most patient with me that summer even when I charged all the windmills that I assumed would prevent the young people I was coming to know and love from being all they could be. "Father Grant," I said, "had seen overly idealistic people like me before, and he would again. But he still gave me his quiet support."

Then I told the congregation about Mrs. Martin, the cook for Head Start, and how she had used her own meager income to feed anyone who was hungry, and how she sat me down, when I was so depressed by all the poverty and what seemed to me the hopelessness of the St. John's neighborhood, and said to me, "Mr. Barnwell, the Lord makes the back to bear the burden."

"Those were the same words," I went on, "that my mother used when comforting me during a difficult time in my life. I learned that long-ago summer from Mrs. Martin and so many others of the many things in our faith and culture, including our old sayings, that can bring us together, instead of letting other things drive us apart."

After I received communion, I returned to my front-row seat next to Mayor Riley and just sat back. I was trying to figure out exactly what this service meant to the new St. John's, to Charleston, and to me. And then I gave up trying to "figure" and just sat there enjoying, imagining that the Old Man, Mother, Pappoo, Aunt Harry, Jimmy Burroughs, Miss Parham, Father Grant, even Dearman, and all those who went before were right there with me. All the love that had been given me over the years was now spilling over for everyone from my past and for everyone right there in that Big Dance-sanctuary.

All shades of whites and blacks, young and old, Episcopalians, Baptists, Pentecostals, Roman Catholics, people from the richest Charleston homes, including the man who in 1966 had called African Americans "Mau-Maus," homeless people—everyone—came up to the altar rail to eat of the same loaf and to drink of the same cup as though that were the most natural thing in the world for people to do. Charleston, I am sure, has just as far to go as any other place in confronting racism and working for justice, farther maybe. For one thing, we need to find ways to claim as our sisters and brothers non-Christians as well as gay men and lesbians, Christian or not, who work in the same vineyard. But, oh my, what a magical night, what a thrilling birthday experience forty-three years after my life-changing summer there in 1966.

Like Jimmy's "last painting"—his funeral in Conway, when he arranged for black and white people to gather *socially* for the first time in that highly segregated town—the consecration of St. John's was a picture of life on the other side and will stay with me for the rest of my life. Had Jesus been there, he would have said, for sure: "And the kingdom of God is like that."

So, life goes on. I must keep on keepin' on, pushin' on, stumblin' on, trying to find my way, our way, to the Promised Land, the place where hostile elements come together. Precious Lord, take my hand. Lead me on, let me stand.

CPSIA information can be obtained
at www.ICGtesting.com
Printed in the USA
BVHW030745220520
579921BV00045B/26